LED CLONES

THE LED ZEPPELIN IMITATOR CRAZE OF THE '80s...AND BEYOND

LED CLONES

THE LED ZEPPELIN IMITATOR CRAZE OF THE '80s...AND BEYOND

BY GREG PRATO

Written by Greg Prato
Printed and distributed by Greg Prato Writer, Corp.
Published by Greg Prato Writer, Corp.
Front cover design by Mary Prato
Front and back cover photos by Christopher Lee Helton
Copyright © 2024, Greg Prato Writer, Corp. All rights reserved. First Edition, October 2024

All rights reserved. No part of this book may be reproduced in any form or by any electronic or mechanical means, including information storage or retrieval systems, without permission in writing from the publisher.

ISBN: 9798342889087

INTRODUCTION

In 1989, rock guitar great Gary Moore issued a tune entitled "Led Clones." Why did this seemingly usually mild-mannered singer/guitarist opt to pen a song with this harsh title? Because he – and also apparently Ozzy Osbourne, who provided lead vocals on the track – had had enough with the onslaught of artists hitting the charts and airwaves that were tremendously influenced by the mighty Led Zeppelin (who had not been a full-time proposition since 1980).

Looking back at '80s rock from the vantage point of when I am typing this (2024), the main styles that proved most popular during that decade were hair metal and mainstream/arena rock, and to a lesser degree, thrash or speed metal – all of which were promoted by MTV. But one movement that seems to be completely forgotten was the Led Zeppelin impersonator craze – a movement which reached its peak during the decade, and in the process, moved quite a few units.

And the list of Zep worshippers was quite lengthy: starting with Billy Squier, continuing into the middle of the decade with the likes of Whitesnake and Great White, before wrapping things up with perhaps the two biggest culprits, Kingdom Come and Bonham before decade's close (heck, even a few alt-rockers got into the act, tops being the Cult). Why are some of these artists oft-overlooked and/or forgotten? Well, perhaps because in some cases, the goal was merely to replicate the sonics and approach of Zeppelin circa 1971, rather than actually *penning songs* that were on par substance-wise with the classic creations by Plant-Page-Jones-Bonham.

But all that said, upon revisiting a few of these artists, some weren't all that bad. And while admittedly it may be a difficult task to sit down and listen to some of their entire discographies – in some cases, even just an *entire album* – a

INTRODUCTION

In 1989, rock guitar great Gary Moore issued a tune entitled "Led Clones." Why did this seemingly usually mild-mannered singer/guitarist opt to pen a song with this harsh title? Because he – and also apparently Ozzy Osbourne, who provided lead vocals on the track – had had enough with the onslaught of artists hitting the charts and airwaves that were tremendously influenced by the mighty Led Zeppelin (who had not been a full-time proposition since 1980).

Looking back at '80s rock from the vantage point of when I am typing this (2024), the main styles that proved most popular during that decade were hair metal and mainstream/arena rock, and to a lesser degree, thrash or speed metal – all of which were promoted by MTV. But one movement that seems to be completely forgotten was the Led Zeppelin impersonator craze – a movement which reached its peak during the decade, and in the process, moved quite a few units.

And the list of Zep worshippers was quite lengthy: starting with Billy Squier, continuing into the middle of the decade with the likes of Whitesnake and Great White, before wrapping things up with perhaps the two biggest culprits, Kingdom Come and Bonham before decade's close (heck, even a few alt-rockers got into the act, tops being the Cult). Why are some of these artists oft-overlooked and/or forgotten? Well, perhaps because in some cases, the goal was merely to replicate the sonics and approach of Zeppelin circa 1971, rather than actually *penning songs* that were on par substance-wise with the classic creations by Plant-Page-Jones-Bonham.

But all that said, upon revisiting a few of these artists, some weren't all that bad. And while admittedly it may be a difficult task to sit down and listen to some of their entire discographies – in some cases, even just an *entire album* – a few of these tunes have aged surprisingly well, or, can be filed neatly into the "guilty pleasure" category. Or, at the very least, select selections that approach "Zep karaoke territory" will bring a smile to your face (hey, at least most of these bands wrote their own tunes, unlike the majority of modern day mainstream pop and rock artists, right?).

And while it's the '80s that is usually pinpointed to as the peak "Led Clone" period, if you really think long and hard about it, it was way back in the early-mid '70s that others (Rush, Heart, Montrose, etc.) began pulling inspiration from the first few Zeppelin albums, and continued to do so for the remainder of the decade. And then fast-forward to the '90s, several grunge bands used Zeppelin as an inspiration (Soundgarden, Nirvana, Stone Temple Pilots, etc.). But unlike many of the '80s Zep disciples, they actually had *the tunes* to back it up – and rather, used Zep as a starting point, before putting their own unique spin on things.

At the time of this book's release, the influence of Zeppelin continues to be felt on a variety of retro-sounding/looking bands – Greta Van Fleet, Rival Sons, Wolfmother, etc. Did these newer models opt to go the way of the '70s, '80s, or '90s Zep-inspired bands? Continue reading to find out!

The song remains the same,
Greg Prato

p.s. Questions? Comments? Feel free to email me at gregprato@yahoo.com.

CONTENTS

Chapter I: What Made Led Zeppelin So Darn Influential?..1
Chapter II: The '70s………………………………………..8
Chapter III: The '80s (Part One)…………………………26
Chapter IV: The '80s (Part Two)…………………………53
Chapter V: The '80s (Part Three)…………………………68
Chapter VI: The '80s (Part Four)…………………………77
Chapter VII: The '80s (Part Five)…………………………90
Chapter VIII: The '90s……………………………………..106
Chapter IX: The 21st Century……………………………134
Chapter X: Zeppelin Cloned Others?……………………..150
Chapter XI: Why So Many in the '80s?…………………..156
Top 50 Tunes……………………………………………160
Sources……………………………………………………162

CHAPTER 1
WHAT MADE LED ZEPPELIN SO DARN INFLUENTIAL?

Arguably, more so than any other decade, the '60s gave us the most influential rock artists of all-time – especially when you are to take into account how many of them did not just influence a single subsequent sub-genre of rock, but rather, countless sub-genres (and continue to do so to this very day). Case in point, the Beatles, the Rolling Stones, Bob Dylan, the Jimi Hendrix Experience, the Grateful Dead, Cream, the Who, the Kinks, Pink Floyd, Sly and the Family Stone, the Allman Brothers Band, the Doors, the Velvet Underground, the Stooges…and of course, Led Zeppelin.

Now, I'm going to assume that if you've chosen to read this little old book, you are already a Zep fan and well-versed in their history. And since the whole point of this is to study their influence – and subsequent "borrowers" of their style – we will not be digging *too* deeply into their history (besides, there have been oodles of other books that thoroughly explore their story). But if I am to attempt to create the most fleeting Led Zep 101 course/summary ever attempted, it would go something like this: session guitarist Jimmy Page joins the Yardbirds in 1966 (first on bass, then on to the six-string), and upon the group's split in 1968, forms the "New Yardbirds" to fulfill previously scheduled shows. His bandmates?

A fellow session player on bass and keyboards, John Paul Jones, and two then-unknowns (and previous bandmates in a joyful band called Band of Joy), Robert Plant and John Bonham, on vocals and drums, respectively. Oh, and I forgot to mention, all hailed from England. By 1969, the band's name had been changed to Led Zeppelin (supposedly after a sly comment made by either the Who's

SO DARN INFLUENTIAL? 2

John Entwistle or Keith Moon), and seemingly almost immediately, became one of the top rock bands in the world.

During their recording career as a functioning band (which would be last from their 1968 inception through 1980, when the band split after Bonham's passing), Zeppelin would issue eight studio albums and one live recording. And in the process, were responsible for many a tune that has been spun countless times on rock radio. In fact, I bet there's a station right now someplace on planet earth that is spinning "Stairway to Heaven," "Whole Lotta Love," "Kashmir," "Black Dog," or "Rock and Roll."

And let me offer a disclaimer before offering the first of what may prove to be several somewhat controversial comments made in this book – I am indeed a great admirer of Zeppelin's music. But they are probably one of the most *overplayed* rock bands in the known universe – to the point that there have been phases were I (and I'm quite certain, other rock fans like me) have gone through long periods of not even being able to listen to a single note of their music, due to severe sonic burnout. However, when I did finally deem my sabbatical over and listened with a fresh set of ears, I was instantly reminded of their greatness and thoroughly enjoyed what I had heard once again.

But what made Zeppelin so darn influential and unique was that they refused to be pinned to a single style. Need some proof? How about touching upon heavy metal ("Whole Lotta Love"), blues ("Since I've Been Loving You"), garage rock ("Communication Breakdown"), folk ("That's the Way"), epics ("Stairway to Heaven"), funk ("Trampled Underfoot"), Middle Eastern sounds ("Kashmir"), reggae ("D'yer Mak'er"), olde tyme rock n' roll ("Boogie with Stu"), jamming the night away (any ol' live rendition of "Dazed and Confused"), country ("Hot Dog"), prog ("Achillies Last Stand"), synth ballads ("All of My

3 LED CLONES

Love"), punk ("Wearing and Tearing"), etc.

And while we're at it, how about a quick look at Zeppelin's discography, album-by-album? 1969's *Led Zeppelin* is often considered one of rock's greatest debuts, and was certainly the group's rawest-sounding recording (a total of *36 hours* is all it took to lay down). Later the same year saw the arrival of *Led Zeppelin II* (probably yours truly's favorite Zep offering of 'em all) which is often looked at as an important stepping stone for what would soon be widely known as "heavy metal." 1970's *Led Zeppelin III* showed that the group was no one-trick pony, as evidenced by its rockin' first side and acoustic second side. 1971's *Led Zeppelin IV* solidified the chaps as one of the world's biggest rock bands – after all, it spawned bloody *"Stairway to Heaven"* (at last count the album has sold 24 million copies...*in the US alone*).

1973's *Houses of the Holy* was another rock classic, while 1975's *Physical Graffiti* merged outtakes from previous albums with new tracks and is often considered one of the greatest rock double-LP's of all-time. 1976's *The Song Remains the Same* is in my humble opinion one of the greatest live rock albums (why it's not more often considered one of the top '70s live albums is one big, giant perplexment).

And their last two offerings, 1976's *Presence* and 1979's *In Through the Out Door*, are often singled out as not being as tip-top as their first six studio documents, but trust me, if you go back and re-listen, there are countless keepers on both. And lastly, the 1982 posthumous release, *Coda*, is best described as a "missed opportunity" to collect odds and ends (especially when such stellar tunes as "Hey, Hey, What Can I Do" and "Travelling Riverside Blues" were not included, and were far better than some of the selections that made the cut). Also, it needs to be mentioned that a single chap produced all of their albums...Jimmy Page.

Although hard to fathom nowadays due to their Ledgendary status, the group was seemingly often scolded in the press during what is now considered their glory days. Especially *Rolling Stone,* who seemed to really have it out for the quartet when it came to reviewing their records, such as that time critic John Mendelsohn said the following about *Zeppelin I*; "It would seem that, if they're to help fill the void created by the demise of Cream, they will have to find a producer (and editor) and some material worthy of their collective attention." Also, while reviewing *Zeppelin III,* Lester Bangs stated, "Unfortunately, precious little of *Z III*'s remaining hysteria is as useful or as effectively melodramatic. 'Friends' has a fine bitter acoustic lead, but gives itself over almost entirely to monotonously shrill Plant breast-beatings. Rob, give a listen to Iggy Stooge."

Or, how about when Jim Miller shared his thoughts on *Physical Graffiti*: "Naturally, *Graffiti* is not without faults — Zeppelin is too intuitive a band to cut a flawless album. Although Page and Bonham mount a bristling attack on 'The Rover,' this track, like several others, suffers from Plant's indefinite pitch. Other cuts, such as the ten-minute 'Kashmir' and 'In My Time of Dying,' succumb to monotony."

All that said – and boy, was it a mouthful – it's not as if Zeppelin magically appeared out of a puff of dry ice and sounded the way they sounded. Just like anyone who has composed music past or present, there were others before them that helped blaze the trail they would eventually trod upon. Most notably, the first two offerings from the Jeff Beck Group, 1968's *Truth* and 1969's *Beck-Ola* (both of which included then-unknowns Rod Stewart and Ron Wood) and such Cream albums as 1967's *Disraeli Gears* and 1968's *Wheels of Fire,* which merged blues with hard rock (and in particular, their song "Politician").

5 LED CLONES

Also, one mustn't forget the high volume and distorted guitar sonics created by such bands as Blue Cheer (and their guitarist, Leigh Stephens) on such tunes as their hit cover of "Summertime Blues," and the Bonzo-like drum bashing that Carmine Appice was heard providing on some of the Vanilla Fudge's numbers. Also, there were certainly a multitude of blues artists (more on that later in the book) that Zeppelin either were influenced by or inserted bits of inside their own tunes – namely Muddy Waters, Howlin' Wolf, and Memphis Minnie, among others.

An additional notable element of Zeppelin was how each member contributed their own "bit" that they would soon become identified with, and, which many of their disciples would soon choose to glom on to:

1. Plant's Golden God/Sex God persona (look, or rather, *listen* no further than the "Ah ah, ah ah, ah ah, ah ah, ah ah, ah ah, ahhh" part of "Black Dog," or his orgasmic cries smack dab in the middle of "Whole Lotta Love"). Although Plant was quoted as once saying, "Bonzo used to say to me, 'Planty, you can't sing. Just go out there, look good and stick your ass out'." I – and a zillion other Zep fans – would beg to differ…Plant could *really* sing.

2. Page's gift for penning goliath guitar riffs, and also, surprisingly gentle acoustic guitar strums, when the mood hit ("A riff ought to be quite hypnotic, because it will be played over and over again," he once explained concerning what makes a great riff).

3. Bonham's powerful drum bashing (and in particular, how his drums were mic'd/recorded in the studio – which we will also discuss in greater detail later).

SO DARN INFLUENTIAL? 6

4. And Jones...well, to be frank, not very many "Zep spawn" mimicked the poor bugger – despite probably being the most musically talented of the bunch (especially if you take into consideration the various instruments he supplied, his composing skills, and later on, playing with and/or producing some impressively musically varied artists).

What also added to the "Zeppelin mystique" were rumors (some of which turned out to be based somewhat in fact) about certain bandmates' over-the-top partying habits with the opposite sex and indulging in certain substances, interest in the supernatural, and intimidation tactics employed by their larger-than-life manager, Peter Grant, and those who handled/helped the group in various capacities. I hate to use a done-to-death cliché, but keep in mind, this was "before the internet and iPhones"...hell, even before bloody MTV. And as a result, teenaged and pre-teen rock fans got most of their info from rock mags, and seemingly most of all from heresy, gossip, and rumors that were untrue, but admittedly, entertaining to pass along, like a classic game of "telephone."

How can anyone forget such infamous tall tales as Frank Zappa and Mick Jagger having an on-stage "gross out" contest? Or how about Rod Stewart ingesting far too much of a certain bodily fluid that afterwards, he had to seek medical attention? What about Gene Simmons having a cow's tongue sewn on to his own already-long appendage for added length? Remember the whole "Paul Is Dead" conspiracy theory concerning Mr. McCartney? Or Stevie Nicks having a special handler that would puff a...you're right, it's best we stop this discussion now. But, you get the idea, I'm sure.

And Zeppelin had several of these stories tied to

7 LED CLONES

them – including an unnatural act with a mud shark and dirty deeds with underaged groupies (consult the lyrics to "Sick Again"), a certain member's admiration of Satan, backwards messages being tucked deep within the grooves of their vinyl LP's, etc. Which, only seemed to add to their mystique and popularity – which resulted in the band ruling the charts and raking up immense album sales, plus also being one of the top-drawing live acts of the '70s (able to headline such vast expanses as Tampa Stadium, the Pontiac Silverdome, and Knebworth, plus multiple nights at Madison Square Garden and the LA Forum).

As a result, when Zeppelin admirably opted to call it quits on December 4, 1980 via a press release – rather than carrying on with a replacement for Bonham (who had passed on September 25th) – a huge void was left in rock music for a similarly-styled act. Which, countless others would soon attempt to fill. However, it turns out that rockers who modeled their own approach and sound after the Zeps reach back further than just the '80s. In fact, it seemed to start while Led Zeppelin was still in business and issuing their iconic recordings, circa the early to mid '70s…

CHAPTER II
THE '70s

Throughout the course of popular music history, whenever an artist becomes massively popular, it's only a matter of time until a slew of similarly-sounding bands crash the scene. And time will tell if some have good intentions – when a selected few eventually locate their own voice and/or original approach – while the majority seem to merely want to make a quick buck and forsake originality. For example, in the wake of Elvis' superstardom came the likes of Fabian, the Beatles spawning a slew of similar sounding/looking British Invasion bands (the Monkees being the most obvious perpetrators), Nirvana "inspiring" the likes of Silverchair, etc.

With Led Zeppelin unquestionably one of the most popular and successful rock bands by the early '70s, the first bands cropped up that had a sound that was decidedly Zep-heavy. And certainly at the top of the list would have to be Rush. Although they would eventually find their own unique sound (peaking with one of the best one-two punches ever in hard rock, 1980's *Permanent Waves* and 1981's *Moving Pictures*), there is no denying that the Canadian trio's self-titled debut from 1974 is pretty much just one giant *Zep-ism*. Case in point, the Robert Plant-esque vocal wailing courtesy of Geddy Lee on such tunes as "Finding My Way" and Alex Lifeson's Jimmy Page-like riffing on "Working Man."

Even Lifeson himself once echoed a similar sentiment – years after the fact. "In the beginning we were labelled as just a lousy Led Zeppelin copy – screeching vocals – and that really stuck with us for a few years. But we kept playing and touring and became much closer with our audience and that's the sort of relationship that we have."

And unlike some artists who fib and pretend as if it's

9 LED CLONES

just one big "happy accident" that they sounded similar (an easy way to wiggle out of a tight spot in an interview has always been, "We share the same influences...so, *of course* we sound similar"), the Rush lads were always honest about being influenced by Zeppelin. And Lee even made sure to admit as much in his superb 2023 autobiography, *My Effin' Life*, when he recalled, "As soon as their first album was released we ran to our local Sam the Record Man, only to find that word was spreading fast and it was already out of stock. When the re-order finally came in, we grabbed one, headed home and laid it on my turntable. I can still remember the three of us sitting there on the bed in utter awe, listening to the heaviosity of 'Good Times Bad Times,' the fire of 'Communication Breakdown,' and oh, that drum sound!"

The bassist didn't just stop there, concerning his praise of Zeppelin and their importance on the development of Rush in his book. "Plant's extreme vocal range and Jimmy's guitar histrionics put this band way over the mark, and for me John Paul Jones's emotionally moving bass lines welded perfectly to the drum parts, grounding the band and creating a rhythm section for a new age of rock. The Who were full of abandon, rockin' hard and melodically brilliant; Jimi [Hendrix] was musical voodoo and flamboyance incarnate; Cream was a showcase of bluesy virtuosity; but this? This was heavy, man. Zep had reforged the blues in an explosive and very English style that would speak to our generation of players like no other. For us there was rock before Zep came along, and there was rock after. This was our new paradigm."

And if that wasn't enough praise and confession of just how important Zeppelin was as a building block for Rush's sound, Lee quite possibly saved the best for last: "Zeppelin challenged the way we felt about our own sound. If it wasn't heavy now, it felt just plain wimpy."

Another time, Rush's singer/bassist also admitted that while listening to Zeppelin on record was one thing, seeing them live on stage was a whole other ballgame. And it just so happened that he didn't have to wait long to experience the might of live Led after hearing their debut album, when he found the required dough (albeit only after pawning his typewriter, which his mother had gifted him!) to secure tickets for their performance at the Rock Pile in Toronto, Canada, on August 18, 1969. Which, for those with a sharp sense of rock history, happened to also fall on the final day of the legendary Woodstock Festival down south in New York (which that morning would have seen Jimi Hendrix's iconic "Star Spangled Banner" performance).

"Musicians talk about life-changing moments and I mean, lots of people talk about life-changing moments. It's hard to take that expression seriously. But I can say in all honesty that for me and Alex Lifeson, my BFF and my partner in crime for a million years, also for John Rutsey who was our drummer at the time, it was a life-changing experience."

"We sat there in the second row and Jimmy Page didn't walk on stage. He *floated* on stage, I'm sure there was a cloud under his feet. It was such a profoundly intense rock experience. The rafters were literally shaking and plaster was literally falling off the ceiling. They really brought the house down. It was a kind of rock music that we had never really heard or felt in that way."

"We went back home as three aspiring young goofs trying to be musicians. We wanted to be like them. So it changed our whole attitude on how we looked at rock music. It really was that profound." When I had the opportunity to ask Lifeson about his memories of attending the Rock Pile gig, he recalled, "We were three rows back on the floor sitting in front of Jimmy Page stage left. They were amazing.

11 LED CLONES

It was a million degrees and after the show we went to a laundromat to dry off our clothes. We sat in there in our underwear."

Fast-forward several years, and it would be one of Rush's most Zep-like tracks that would lead to their first "hit" within the US rock radio market, when DJ Donna Halper played "Working Man" on WMMS in Cleveland, Ohio. "I was up in my office and I was listening to the new music. We were deciding what we were gonna play that week, and suddenly, I get this thing from Canada."

"And I remember dropping the needle on what was the longest cut, because back in those days in album rock, you were always looking for what was called 'bathroom songs.' And a bathroom song was something that if you did have to answer the call of nature, the record wouldn't run out. And then I start listening to the song, and I'm just, 'Oh my God, this is a perfect record for Cleveland.' Back then, it was a factory town. The song 'Working Man,' every listener in the audience felt like that."

"Phones light up immediately – 'When's the new Led Zeppelin album out?' 'No, no, not a new Led Zeppelin album. Canadian band. Rush.' Every time the record gets played people are calling, 'Where can we get one? Where can we get one'?"

However, when I had the opportunity to ask Lifeson about "Working Man" for my 2023 eBook, *The 100 Greatest Songs of Heavy Metal* (oops, guess I just gave away one of the list's lucky selections!), he explained that it was not Zeppelin that inspired the track, but rather, another legendary British band. "'Working Man' was written in the early 1970s when we were 17 years old. Influenced by our love for Cream, it became one of our longer jam songs and an opportunity to stretch out and exhaust our teenage fingers. Working kids, indeed!"

Another time, Lee would admit that John Paul Jones' bass playing on the Zep classic "What Is and What Should Never Be" proved to be an enormous influence, as well. "There are so many songs I could choose from Zep that feature profound but understated bass playing, but this one is my fave. The way John Paul Jones changes gear, holds down the heavy bottom and adds terrific melody throughout the song. He is such a fluid player and all-round musical talent."

And there's a happy ending to this story – upon the exit of the drummer that provided the backbeat on their '74 debut, John Rutsey, Rush's direction was instantly shifted with the arrival of his replacement. Of course, I'm talkin' 'bout Neil Ellwood Peart – whose arrival steered the group towards a more challenging prog-metal direction, and also, improved the group's lyrics tremendously (as he would provide most of the group's lyrics from 1974's *Fly By Night* onward).

Looking back upon Canadian rock bands of the '70s, it seems like the majority were equally influenced by Zep rock and also, prog rock. And a fellow Canadian rocker, Rik Emmett – whose band, Triumph, was a contemporary of Rush – explained why/how this occurred. "I think the prog thing came just a tiny bit later. But if you look back on Zeppelin, their first album came out in North America in '69, their second album came out in '69, their third album came out in '70, their fourth album came out in '71. So, in two years you got four albums. That's like *a blizzard* of stuff."

"And at the same time, you had all these other acts that were doing stuff like, the Jeff Beck *Truth* album was '68 – that was a very influential album here. Pink Floyd albums were happening at the same time. Right around then I was discovering Yes, Genesis, and Pink Floyd. Canadian radio – that was a lot of the stuff they played. So, there was a big

13 LED CLONES

market for that stuff in Canada. But the thing of course was...*it was a little harder to play*. [Laughs] You needed more gear, you needed more musicians. It was a long haul between gigs in Canada, so that's why it was more like, 'Keep the band small. Make it be a trio – you can all fit in the van with the gear'."

"I think it's fair to say that the whole idea of 'riff rocking' was kind of the thing that Zeppelin figured out. I liked Deep Purple a lot, but you had to lug around a Hammond B3. If you were trying to get in at the grass roots and you were a power trio, it was just a question of having amps on the backline – and you didn't have to have a fourth guy to pay. So, Zeppelin, Hendrix, and Cream – that was the triumvirate of heavy bands that everybody said, 'We can do this. The least amount of mouths to feed, and the most amount of noise you could make'."

Another one of the earliest Zep disciples to hit the scene in the early '70s was Montrose – led by guitarist Ronnie Montrose, and a then-unknown Sammy Hagar on lead vocals. Hailing from the Bay Area of California, quite a bit of their classic self-titled debut from 1973 (which was produced by Ted Templeman, who would later oversee many a classic Van Halen recording) contained material that was certainly Zep-like – most noticeably in the guitar work of Montrose and within the beefy beats provided by drummer Denny Carmassi.

But unlike Geddy Lee's vocals in Rush, Hagar's singing in Montrose was not Plant-esque at all, which made such standouts as "Rock the Nation," "Bad Motor Scooter," and "Space Station #5" not as obviously Zep-derivative as say, Rush's "Finding My Way," "Working Man," or "What You're Doing." But the same could not be said for the tune "Rock Candy," which is a 100% glorious Zep rip (again, especially in the Page-like riffing and Bonham-sounding drum beats), with the album-closer "Make It Last" coming in second place. And despite the LP being – rightly – considered a rock classic and the future appearing quite bright for the band, the Hagar-fronted version of Montrose would last for only one more album (1974's not-as-good *Paper Money*), before the Red Rocker rocked elsewhere.

Back in the good ol' days when I was writing for *Rolling Stone*, I had the opportunity to speak to Hagar shortly after Ronnie Montrose's passing on March 3, 2012. And I'll let you in on a little secret: although the article was credited solely to Hagar, it was yours truly who conducted the interview and shaped it into an article. And during his tribute, he shed quite a bit of light on this era of Montrose, including admitting that:

"The first Montrose album was the first album I ever recorded and it still stands as one of the best recordings I have ever been a part of. I wrote songs with [Montrose], but it was his trip. He's the guy that got me to sing with him. I had no experience whatsoever; I just wrote the first four songs in my life, which were 'Bad Motor Scooter,' 'Make It Last,' 'One Thing on My Mind,' and 'I Don't Want It,' played them for Ronnie upon first meeting, shook my hand, and said, 'Let's start a band.' I went from zero to a hundred."

Hagar would go on to recount that seeing Montrose play a show while the guitarist was a member of the Edgar Winter Group at Winterland in San Francisco not only inspired him to split up the band he was in at the time (which was more soul than rock), but ultimately, to pay Montrose an unannounced visit shortly afterward.

"I went and knocked on his door, dressed like David Bowie – big old high heel platform shoes, satin pants, probably had make-up on, with a Les Paul and a notebook pad with all kinds of lyrics in it. I said, 'I'm Sammy Hagar. I heard you're looking for a singer.' He said, 'Come on in. You

15 LED CLONES

got any songs?' I played him my four songs, we shook hands, and he said, 'Let's start a band. Do you know any drummers? I've got a bass player, Bill Church.' I had a drummer, Denny Carmassi – wasn't in my band, but he was my favorite drummer around town. Within a month we were signed to Warner Bros. Records, Ted Templeman producing, and the first Montrose album was born a month after that. It was the fastest thing I've ever done in my life. Like I said, I went from zero to a hundred in the blink of an eye – all because of Ronnie."

And lastly, Hagar also explained why the band would soon splinter – even after issuing such a classic rock recording right from the get-go. "We made one of the greatest hard rock/heavy metal albums of all-time with that first Montrose album, and then he didn't want to do that anymore. 'Nah, nah, we've got to have better songs, we've got to change our image, that kind of music is out.' Boy, he was just laying it on us. Ronnie really liked to change – immediately. We butted heads and I got thrown out of the band [after *Paper Money*], but I carried on with that 'first Ronnie Montrose' I saw."

And while most of the artists influenced by Zeppelin past and present turned out to be male, there was at least one exception. Of course, the artist in question is Heart. Hailing from Vancouver, British Columbia (boy, Zep certainly left an impression on Canadians, eh?), the group was led by sisters Ann Wilson on vocals and Nancy Wilson on guitar, and like Montrose, issued a classic debut straight away, with 1975's *Dreamboat Annie* – which spawned such hits as "Magic Man" and "Crazy on You."

"There were no female influences really," Nancy once admitted. "When we first saw the Beatles, we wanted to be in the band. Then when we saw Zeppelin, we wanted to be Zeppelin. I was channeling Jimmy Page, and Elton

John's piano playing on acoustic guitar. Ann was channeling Robert Plant and Paul Rodgers. Guys like Robert Plant looked like really hot chicks, and we felt like we could be hot chicks or hot dudes on a big rock stage like that. Androgyny and a sense of humor were our basic survival tools, because there was no place for us at the time."

And unlike the aforementioned Montrose, Heart's music overall was not an obvious tip o' the cap to Zeppelin…until you came across a specific track. And that track was "Barracuda," off their third offering, 1977's *Little Queen*, which contained more than a passing resemblance riff and groove-wise (as well as sonically) to Zeppelin's "Achilles Last Stand."

However, Nancy once discussed the creation of the riff, which was indeed inspired by a '70s hard rock band…but not the one we all think. "We'd been opening for a band called Nazareth in Europe, and also for Queen. And Nazareth had a hit with a Joni Mitchell song that they'd covered, 'This Flight Tonight,' that kind of riff [sings 'Barracuda' riff]. So, we kind of borrowed that and we made it into 'Barracuda.' And then we saw the guys from Nazareth later, and they were *pissed*. 'You took our riff!' But…you borrow from what you love and you make it your own. But it's one of those sounds, too – guitar tones – that I'm still trying to figure out what we did. Because it's hard to recreate."

And concerning the song's title and lyrics, Ann was also willing to set the record straight – during a conversation with renowned headbanger Dan Rather. "'Barracuda' was just a moment…it was a flash of anger. A realization of what we had gotten ourselves into. It happened one night after a show, some really sleazy guy came up to me and implied to me that he was 'really turned on' by the fact that Nance and me were lesbian incestual lovers. And that just 'really got

17 LED CLONES

him going.' In his fantasy."

"That made me *so* mad, because I love my sister and suddenly, my mother's face came right up, saying, 'Don't get into show business. It's so tacky. It's so full of sleazy people that are going to misunderstand you.' And I went, 'Oh, *you're so right*.' It made me really angry – especially because I felt that they had attacked her honor…both our honors. So, I went and wrote the words to 'Barracuda.' I think if I had a gun, I would have reacted differently to the guy…but thank goodness I didn't."

There would also be several other ties between Heart and the Zepsters over the years – including covering "Rock and Roll" live (and included on their 1980 release *Greatest Hits/Live*), the Wilson sisters doing battle with "The Battle of Evermore" under the guise of the Lovemongers (for 1992's *Singles Motion Picture Soundtrack*), and most obvious of all, once performing "Stairway to Heaven" with John Bonham's son, Jason, on drums.

And it turns out that the occasion for covering the most hallowed and untouchable of all Zep tunes was a special one – when all three surviving members of Led Zeppelin attended the Kennedy Center Honors on December 2, 2012, during a ceremony in which they were being…honored. Heart's rendition seems to have taken on "Queen at Live Aid" proportions over the years – concerning how universally praised it has become. And it turns out that Nancy received the highest compliment later that evening.

"Jimmy Page came up later and said, 'Wow, I love the way you play that song.' I was like, 'God, I could die now.' I was just in shock to hear that coming out of him. Then Plant said, 'I've really come to hate that song. But wow, you guys did a great job.' Jimmy Page telling me he thought I played great was so incredibly life-altering! It made me want to get better. Keep working it!"

And while I'd elect Rush, Montrose, and Heart as probably the three most celebrated Zep-sounders of the '70s, there were certainly quite a few others that never seem to get mentioned in the conversation nearly as much. One of which, would be the just-mentioned Queen. Perhaps the most musically varied rock band of all-time, Queen – particularly early on – certainly had their Zep-y moments. And one tune in particular off their 1973 self-titled debut bore a resemblance riff-wise – which kicked off side 2 of the vinyl version, "Liar."

When interviewing Twisted Sister singer Dee Snider for the 2018 book, *Long Live Queen: Rock Royalty Discuss Freddie, Brian, John & Roger*, he explained how the first time he heard the aforementioned tune, thinking it was a certain band that enjoyed singing about lemons, Vikings, and hedgerows. "I am a 'day one/original Queen fan' – when there were *no* American Queen fans. I was right out of the gate. I heard them on WNEW [a New York radio station]. I was working a day job, and they played 'Liar,' off the first album. It was this DJ, Jonathan Schwartz, and he hosted a show called *Things from England*, and once a week, he would play something new. I was like, 'What the fuck…who is that?' First when I heard the song, I thought it was Yes, I thought it was Led Zeppelin…who is it? *'It's Queen'.*"

Also in the same book, Anthrax guitarist Scott Ian could hear the connection between Queen and Zeppelin during a specific phase of their recording career. "You go back to some of their earlier stuff, and it was very Zeppelin-influenced, obviously – not that there's anything wrong with that – but what about 'Seven Seas of Rhye'? What a sick song."

And at various other points of Queen's studio recordings with legendary vocalist Freddie Mercury, there were further zaps of Zep – namely several extended/epic

19 LED CLONES

tunes, including "It's Late" (whose riff 16 seconds in bears some resemblance to "Ten Years Gone") and "Innuendo" (which may or may not contain some nods to "Kashmir"…after all, this was one of the tunes that R. Plant sang with Queen at the Freddie Mercury Tribute Concert in 1992).

Another band who has been known to break out a Zep riff and/or drum beat when the situation called for it was Long Island sci-fi metallists Blue Öyster Cult. And one BÖC tune that I always felt fell neatly into this category was "Cities on Flame with Rock and Roll," off their oft-overlooked 1972 self-titled debut. But while chatting with original BÖC drummer Albert Bouchard for the 2020 book *BONZO: 30 Rock Drummers Remember the Legendary John Bonham*, he set me straight.

"If it did it was completely subconscious, because there were other drummers that I was imitating on that song – like the James Gang's Jimmy Fox. I kind of was imitating him and I was also imitating [Black Sabbath's] Bill Ward. And I was also imitating the guy on the first King Crimson record [Michael Giles is the drummer on 1969's *In the Court of the Crimson King*]. Actually, a song that I sort of consciously imitated Bonham would be the song 'Nosferatu' on *Spectres*. I actually play the 'Good Times Bad Times' fill in the middle. But even just the demo feel of that one, I felt like a Bonham kind of a thing would go well, and would be a juxtaposition – it's not a blues-based thing, it's more like a gothic kind of epic thing. But maybe more like Zeppelin towards the end of their career."

Another aspect of BÖC's approach which I felt may have crossed into Zep terrain was Bonzo's use of cowbell in "Good Times Bad Times" – which just might have led to Bouchard infamously clanking a cowbell in "(Don't Fear) The Reaper." But once more, my theory was shot to shit.

Bouchard: "I'd love to say, 'Yes! That's exactly where we got it!' But no – not at all. It wasn't even my idea – it was [producer] David Lucas. David felt that it needed more...that drum part was really imitating [the Byrds'] Mike Clarke."

"Donald said, 'Can you play me a beat that's kind of a Byrds song?' I said, 'You mean like Mike Clarke plays? You mean a totally 'white boy' beat?' He goes, 'Yes! Yes! That's it! No funk! No funk!' And the cowbell part was David Lucas' idea – I fought him on it, too. I was like, 'Really? I don't think it sounds good, Dave.' And he says, 'No, no. It will sound good. Don't worry'." A good thing Bouchard didn't worry, because it led to perhaps the best known use of a cowbell ever in a rock song (thanks to a certain *Saturday Night Live* skit starring Christopher Walken).

Another rock act that certainly had their Zep moments was Boston's finest, Aerosmith. No, not their stinky latter power ballad phase, I mean their '70s drug-festooned high point, and in particular, such classic albums as 1975's *Toys in the Attic* and 1976's *Rocks*. And probably the best example of this was the gonzo riff featured within the *Attic* deep cut, "Round and Round" (just how deep? How about the second to last song of the LP!). And it turns out that the tune – not to be confused with the Ratt tune of the same name – was crafted by none other than guitarist Brad Whitford, rather than Joe Perry. "I don't remember a whole lot about this one," Whitford once admitted. "I just remember being in the Record Plant, and I had the main riff of that song. It was one of those riffs that everybody said, 'We've got to do something with that.' It turned into quite a production."

A second Aero composition that includes an element of Zep is one of their best known tunes, "Sweet Emotion." And I don't mean probably the best known part of the tune (its opening bassline by Tom Hamilton), but rather, the

21 LED CLONES

heavy part that wallops you directly on the noggin at the 1:15 mark. And a third and final 'smith song that oozes a bit of Led is another deep cut, "Nobody's Fault," off *Rocks*. And it's not the guitar nor vocal that is reminiscent of Zeppelin, but rather, the *enormous sound* of the recording, and also, the tempo provided by drummer Joey Kramer.

Now, at this point of the chapter, how about we discuss one of the more obscure Zep replicators of the '70s – another Canadian band (see, *what did I tell you* about the Great White North's affection for the band) that went by the name of Moxy. Never heard of them? Don't feel bad, neither did I – until I heard a couple of their tunes nestled within the 1989 Tommy Bolin box set, *The Ultimate* (as Bolin was hired as a session guitarist to lend his six-string skills to several tunes on their 1975 self-titled debut). And upon giving the entire album a listen, tunes such as "Can't You See I'm a Star," "Still I Wonder," and "Out of the Darkness – Into the Fire" contain undeniable Zep elements. But one tune in particular, "Train," is the group's most obvious swipe.

Speaking to Moxy guitarist Earl Johnson for the 2008 book, *Touched by Magic: The Tommy Bolin Story*, he explained how the late/great guitarist (best known for short stints in the James Gang and Deep Purple, plus playing on the jazz-fusion classic *Spectrum* by Billy Cobham) got involved with the band in the studio. "I loved his playing, but never met him personally, and wish I had. I wrote about 95% of Moxy's first album as the guitar player. I got into a fight with the producer about the guitar solos I was playing at the time – more like Page and Beck – and Tommy was brought in one night when I was thrown out of the studio by the producer."

Looking back years later, Johnson figures it all worked out for the best. "It actually made me a better player, as I felt challenged, and knew I had to improve my playing.

Tommy had a great feel and style, and I admired him for that. Moxy went on to record two more albums, and by the third album, I was ripping and completely confident – much of that was derivative from the first album. I was lucky in that our two biggest songs from the first album were songs that I played all the guitar tracks on – 'Sail On Sail Away' and 'Can't You See I'm A Star'."

However, Bolin's brother, Johnnie, had mixed feelings about Tommy's involvement in the project. "He did that because they paid him in coke. That's all he remembered about it. He played good on that though. That song 'Train,' that's not even Tommy playing that guitar solo. Really listen to it – put on any track before that or any track of Tommy's. He does the first part of the solo, but the actual solo itself is not him – it's the other guy."

And yet *another* Canadian band that also got "Zepped" was the aforementioned Triumph. And their singer/guitarist, Rik Emmett, has clear memories of Zeppelin's early influence on him as a musician. "I can remember sitting in the living room with the Zeppelin albums – moving the needle, moving the needle – trying to figure out, 'How do you play that intro to 'Black Dog'?' Which now, everybody knows what it is. But back in those days, *nobody* knew – 'How do you count that thing? That's just weird.' Everybody played it wrong. To model ourselves after Zeppelin was the thing that allowed us to get our foot inside the door and have a professional career."

As a result, there are certain early Triumph tunes that have an unmistakable "Led flavor" to them. "If you listen to the first Triumph album [1976's self-titled], there were 'riff rock' songs. Songs like 'Be My Lover,' there is an amalgam of influences that show up. But the riffs would be 'Be My Lover,' 'Easy Life' – *that's Zeppelin*. And the proof in the pudding was in those days, we were still a bar band, and we

23 LED CLONES

still played two sets of Led Zeppelin every night."

"That was kind of what we were known for – we had these 'Zeppelin medleys.' We'd come up on stage and we'd play nothing but Zeppelin songs for 45 minutes. Then we'd go back to the dressing room and come out and play another set of Zeppelin stuff for about half an hour. It became a thing where club owners said, 'Oh…are you going to come and do your 'Led Zeppelin show'?' We had pretty good versions of 'Whole Lotta Love,' 'Stairway to Heaven,' 'Black Dog,' 'Heartbreaker,' and all that kind of stuff."

Emmett even admitted that Zeppelin had an influence on Triumph's eventual live performances, as well. "We bought a theremin and we fiddled around with it. [Laughs] Mike Levine had a keyboard rack like John Paul Jones. There were all kinds of things that were formative things for us that came from going, 'Well…*Zeppelin does this.*' The 'Heartbreaker' solo that Jimmy Page played, when Triumph did *Rock & Roll Machine*, the 'Rock & Roll Machine' solo was a staple of the Triumph show the entire career – 'Rik would do a guitar solo.' And then when Eddie Van Halen did 'Eruption,' it was like, 'Oh…*the rule book just got rewritten.*'

Elsewhere in the '70s, there were certainly other renowned rockers who took a sip from the Zep water fountain at various points. Masked rockers Kiss were always quite vocal in the press about their admiration of Zeppelin, but truth be told, not very many of their songs reflected this (1976's "Makin' Love" probably came closest). But with the release of their 1977 double disc, *Alive II*, that all changed in a jiffy – in particular, five newly-recorded studio tracks on side four.

While Kiss' Peter Criss was a solid drummer (and often credited as an influence on countless subsequent rock time keepers), his playing was closer to the Charlie Watts style of drumming rather than to Bonham. But on the tune "Larger Than Life," Criss does his best Bonzo, while session guitarist Bob Kulick (filling in on for the suddenly far-too-busy Ace Frehley) offers some simply fantastic Page-like guitar noodling. And it certainly didn't hurt that a gentleman who engineered several Zep albums, Eddie Kramer, was producing, and that the band really "explored the space" of the Capitol Theatre in Passaic, New Jersey, where the material was recorded (sans audience).

Additionally, quite a few southern rockers of the decade offered up songs with a few righteous riffs on par with the kind that James Patrick Page was cooking up around the same time – Lynyrd Skynyrd's "Gimme Back My Bullets" and "I Ain't the One," ZZ Top's "Precious and Grace" and "Just Got Paid." Also, let's not forget Zep's labelmates on their own Swan Song Records, Bad Company, and the riff featured on "Feel Like Makin' Love." And also a few of Zep's '70s peers who sounded similar: Cactus' "One Way…or Another," Beck, Bogert & Appice's "Black Cat Moan," Funkadelic's "Alice in My Fantasies," T. Rex's "20th Century Boy," Kansas' "Carry on Wayward Son," Tommy Bolin's "Shake the Devil," and Alice Cooper's "It's Hot Tonight," among others.

"I loved all that stuff," said radio personality (and co-host of *That Metal Show*) Eddie Trunk, concerning the '70s bands that Zepped the night away. "I think there's a big difference between being influenced by music that came before and blatantly ripping it off or sounding like it. To my ears, I thought that there's an obvious influence with the bands you mentioned [Rush, Heart, and Montrose]. But I didn't think it was blatant."

"That first Rush album, I *still* love that record. And it is a 'big riff record.' And obviously, there's a Zeppelin feel to it – no doubt. I didn't feel like it was, 'Oh, these guys are

25 LED CLONES

blatantly ripping off Zeppelin.' I just felt like Zeppelin were the kings and they had a lot of influence, but I did feel like those bands were doing their own thing. When you look at Heart, the acoustic elements definitely come from Zeppelin. And Ann's voice, as big as it is – you can make that comparison obviously with Robert Plant."

"And the big thing with Rush with the first record is that Neil Peart wasn't on it. So, Rush grew up with Cream, Zeppelin, the Who, and stuff like that. So, that's where they were at – at that time as kids. And then Neil coming in on the second record, everything changed – that's when Neil started writing and it became more of a progressive thing. To me, it was – no pun intended – Rush 'finding their way' on the first record."

However, with the arrival of such back-to-basics styles as punk rock and new wave apparently shifting the direction of rock towards the close of the '70s (and over in the UK, the New Wave of British Heavy Metal movement also bringing metal closer to the punk side of things), it would be understandable to assume that Led Zeppelin's influence on rock bands may be winding down. Little did we know…*it was just beginning.*

CHAPTER III
THE '80s (PART ONE)

Led Zeppelin entered the '80s seemingly back on track. Having taken a sabbatical from touring (after the tragic death of Robert Plant's young son, Karac, in 1977), the group had reconvened for a new album in 1979, *In Through the Out Door*, and a handful of shows. But in 1980, they were aiming to ramp up the amount of touring considerably – with a run of Euro dates in the summer, and the group's first North American tour in three years set to start in October. But then, tragedy struck again – when John Bonham died on September 25th (at the age of 32), just as rehearsals had begun for the autumn dates.

On December 4, 1980, a press release was issued confirming that Zeppelin was no more. And just like that, a ginormous void was left in rock music. But just as quickly as you could say "a bustle in your hedgerow," there were seemingly countless artists issuing albums that were *heavily* Zep derivative. And even exacerbating the void further was when Robert Plant and Jimmy Page launched their first initial post-Zep projects and began touring (Plant as a solo artist and Page as part of the all-star ARMS Charity Concerts and then as a member of the Firm, which teamed him with ex-Bad Company singer Paul Rodgers), both made it a point to play no material from their former band – besides Page playing an instrumental version of "Stairway to Heaven" during the ARMS era.

Now, if there was one band that ever came close to filling the aforementioned void, it was the only one that I could deem "the American Led Zeppelin" with a straight face, and they even managed to do it *without* shamelessly aping them – Van Halen. Sure, David Lee Roth was not the vocal talent that Plant was, bassist Michael Anthony was not

27 LED CLONES

the multi-instrumentalist JPJ was, and while a powerhouse drummer, Alex Van Halen was not exactly on par with Bonzo, Eddie Van Halen simply *revolutionized* rock guitar.

And as many VH connoisseurs are aware, it was what he saw at a Led Zeppelin concert that led to a young Edward experimenting with placing two hands on the fretboard, and coming up shortly thereafter with his trademark "two hand tapping" technique. "I'll never forget, Alex and I used to go to every concert at the Forum in LA, and Led Zeppelin is playing, and Jimmy Page is going like this...he's going [plays guitar]. But he's got his hand up in the air! Basically, I just moved the nut to get this part – here's the nut. But then, instead of using this hand, I use this hand so you can't tell which finger I'm using."

However, Eddie was not always exceedingly complimentary towards Page's playing, as he was once quoted as saying, "Jimmy Page is an excellent producer. *Led Zeppelin* and *Led Zeppelin II* are classics. As a player, he's very good in the studio. But I never saw him play well live. He's very sloppy. He plays like he's got a broken hand and he's two years old. But if you put out a good album and play like a two-year-old live, what's the purpose?" Interestingly, this quote was from January 1981 – a point at which Page's guitar skills had not noticeably slipped when compared to later in the decade (at two high profile Zep one-off reunions), where such a scathing critique may have made more sense. More on that later.

But back to Zep's influence on VH – during the band's definitive Roth era (1978-1984), there weren't many obvious detours into Zep land. But I always felt that "In a Simple Rhyme" had its Zep moments (particularly the opening 12-string bit), Alex provided an unmistakably Bonzo-sounding beat on "Sunday Afternoon in the Park," etc. And of course, there was no denying that Roth took

Plant's sex god/golden god shtick and pumped it up on steroids (as evidenced by his flamboyant on-stage fashion sense – including wearing leather chaps with his bare toches exposed) plus sometimes spicy on-stage banter. In fact, you could probably make the argument that VH became much more well-versed in Zep-isms with the arrival of former Montrose singer Sammy Hagar in 1985 – most obviously detected in the drums and overall vibe of such ditties as "Poundcake," "Man on a Mission," and "The Seventh Seal."

And during the '80s, if you were to select a "UK counterpart" to Van Halen as far as popularity and also having a few Zep components to their sound, Def Leppard would probably fit the bill best. Perhaps the similarities between both bands weren't even musical – the spelling of Def Leppard's name was obviously modeled after Led Zeppelin's. Additionally, guitarist Steve Clark's fondness for playing low-slung Gibson Les Pauls a la Señor Page (and as evidenced by a photo within this book, even a double neck Gibson, straight outta "Stairway to Heaven"). Also, in a video promoting the 40th anniversary edition of their breakthrough album, *Pyromania*, Lep bassist Rick Savage discussed the song "Rock of Ages," and admitted that "I think it's fair to say that the initial inspiration for the track was actually 'In the Evening' by Led Zeppelin."

However, to Leppard's credit, their fondness for Zep never overtook their own style/sound, which – for better or for worse – became the industry standard from *Pyromania* on throughout the '80s. In case you have no clue what I mean, let me clear it up – their fondness for choir-like backing vocals, triggered/electronic-sounding drums, the grand production courtesy of super-producer Mutt Lange, etc. So if anything, Def Leppard were *Queen* disciples, rather than *Zep* disciples. But still, there were certain Zep = Lep moments, particularly in the pre-Lange era of the band.

29 LED CLONES

Namely, the riffs in the tunes "Rocks Off" and "It Don't Matter." Additionally, renowned rock photographer Mark Weiss could also hear a similarity, when he pointed out in the book *MTV Ruled the World: The Early Years of Music Video*, "I thought [Def Leppard] was a slicker version of Led Zeppelin."

Another band that had a few Zep-worthy riffs in their repertoire was the Dixie Dregs (aka simply, the Dregs). An all-instrumental band led by fleet-fingered guitarist Steve Morse – and including a pre-Winger Rod Morgenstein on drums – a tune like the awesomely-titled "Bloodsucking Leeches" (off 1982's *Industry Standard*) certainly contains a meaty riff that sounds unmistakably Page-like. However, one thing that tends to hamper the Dregs is their production is often squeaky clean – the complete opposite of the type of dirt n' grime that such tunes as Zep's "The Rover" or "The Wanton Song" kicked up, and made them so dang irresistible.

In fact, Morse once selected Led Zeppelin's self-titled debut as one of his "10 Records That Changed My Life" for *Classic Rock Magazine*, and admitted, "This album made a big impression on me. Jimmy Page's riffs, his arrangements, his production – such overall talent. But he also had a lot of restraint. He didn't pile everything on all the time; he would bring something in here and there, steel guitar parts, and put it all together in just the right way. That really made a lot of sense to me as a teenager."

But the first *true* Zep mimic of the '80s would have to be Billy Squier. First hitting the record store racks as a member of obscure late '70s rockers Piper, the band issued just a pair of albums (1976's self-titled debut and 1977's *Can't Wait*), before going the way of the dodo. Securing his own solo deal shortly thereafter, Squier opened the '80s with the so-so *The Tale of the Tape* in 1980, which spawned the song "The Big Beat" – parts of which would later be sampled by some of the biggest hip-hop artists known to mankind (Jay-Z, Ice Cube, Run-DMC, etc.).

But it was with the arrival of 1981's *Don't Say No*, that Squier went all Zeppelin-y on us – both in the sonic and songwriting departments. And it sounds like hooking up with Queen's then-producer, Mack (full-name: Reinhold Mack), was what set him on a direct path towards the houses of the holy.

"I was going to do my first solo album with [Queen guitarist] Brian May as producer; he's an old friend, and he said: 'I want to do it but we've got to have Mack involved' – Queen had just started working with him at this stage," explained Squier at the time. "And that made me think, because Brian's very fastidious and not easily impressed. I asked who Mack was and he said, 'Oh, he's the guy behind all those ELO records,' and I went, 'God, he did them? Say no more,' because sound-wise they're fantastic, very clever and dynamic."

"As it turned out, Brian couldn't do the album because he didn't have enough time, so last year, when I was preparing to start work on *Don't Say No*, I just thought of Mack. I rang him up, we met, and it all went from there." And as the bassist on *Don't Say No*, Mark Clarke, recalled in 2024, "There was so much momentum from the record company, and the band was really great. [Drummer] Bobby Chouinard – 'Mr. Big Beat' – was always so upbeat. He had his problems, but we always forgave him and he drove it all. Bobby and I really kicked the whole bottom end in. It was thoroughly enjoyable. We did that in a matter of weeks – we did that *whole* album."

"Mack was one of the best engineers – still to this day – that I've ever worked with," Clarke continues. "Geoff Emerick was another one of them – who did all the Beatles

31 LED CLONES

stuff. You'd go into the studio with Geoff, and you'd play in the studio and it sounds great. Most engineers, when you went back into the control room and listened back to it, you would say, 'It doesn't sound like that in the studio.' Geoff and Mack, when you walked back into the control room, it sounded way more powerful than it did in the actual studio. And that's what Mack brought. And Mack would make very quiet suggestions."

Out of all the Led Clones past and present, the best album front to back quality and sonically-wise is quite possibly this LP, as Squier appears to have modeled it after the direction and production of the last two Zep studio LP's – *Presence* and *In Through the Out Door* – rather than the era most swiped from by others (1969-1975). For example, once the tune "Lonely Is the Night" kicks in at the 34 second mark, it sounds oh-so-close to Zep's "Nobody's Fault But Mine." And the merger of synths or keyboards into the hard rock of "In the Dark" and "The Stroke" sounds not a million miles away from "In the Evening" and "Carouselambra" (the latter which is my personal choice for one of Zep's most underrated tunes).

Clarke also remembers learning the news of a tragedy in the middle of recording one of the album's aforementioned classics. "The night that we did 'In the Dark' was the night that John Lennon got shot [December 8, 1980]. We were doing it at the Power Station in New York. I went out in the reception area, and Billy is over there with everyone else watching television – *totally* in shock. Because of my Beatles connection [Clarke hails from Liverpool], he said, 'Do you want to stop?' I said, 'No, I don't want to stop. Let's carry on.' We did call it quits at about 2:00 or 3:00 in the morning. Billy and I lived very close to each other on the Upper West Side – I lived only about two blocks from the Dakota, and Billy was about four blocks away. So, the limo arrived at the studio to take us home, and the driver said, 'We can't got up the West Side because of what's happened.' I'll never forget that."

Vocally, while Squier doesn't scream and wail like Plant at his horniest, it wouldn't take much effort to picture the Golden God easily slipping into such tunes as "My Kinda Lover." And like Zeppelin, Squier was going for a "tight but loose" vibe throughout – in other words, feel rather than a technically perfect take. "I like to keep the bass and drums as live as possible and a lot of the time the loosest takes are the best," Squier admitted back in the '80s. "I remember when we recorded 'Too Daze Gone' for *Don't Say No*. We did it at about five in the morning and it was really sloppy, but it had the right feel, so we used it'."

But besides Squier, it was his drummer who was the co-star of the show, Bobby Chouinard. Who, as heard throughout the album, was one of the few '80s era rock drummers that was able to recreate the power, feel, and sound of the then-recently-deceased Bonham. "Bobby was really able to imitate Bonzo's attitude," Mountain drummer Corky Laing once pointed out. "He had that 'space thing' going with a snare and his bass drum. He played like...*a pubic hair* behind the backbeat – which gave it that sexy kind of thing. And there are a few guys that do that."

"That was Mack's influence," added Mark Clarke, concerning Squier's then-drummer. "And also, Bobby had a style. I'm sure if Bonzo would have heard Bobby, he would have loved him. There was just something about Bobby that, I can't say he was a technical genius, but he had 'the feel.' It was an amazing, simple technique he had. And he also had a big bass drum that Bonzo used to use. Yeah, Bobby was a freakin' *loud* drummer. Even on a simple 2/4 beat, he was killing it."

And unlike some musicians who lose their cool when

33 LED CLONES

asked the tough questions, you have to admire Squier's response in a 1984 interview with *Kerrang!*, when writer Mick Wall asked, "You must have heard it said Billy Squier is Jimmy Page and Robert Plant rolled into one. Does that piss you off?"

"Well, I try to take it as a great compliment, but it doesn't do justice to me or them," he replied. "All journalists are into comparisons, they have to be if they're trying to depict something as abstract and intangible as music. But nobody has ever compared my songwriting to Robert Plant's. If they did, they'd have to be writing for themselves in some attic, because it's a ludicrous comparison."

"I don't mind if people want to compare my voice to Robert's, although I don't think I do sound like him. What I do is not an attempt to be Robert. What I do is not an attempt to be Rod Stewart, and I get compared to him too – but fuck it, that's good company I'm keeping. I learned from them, I'll tell ya that: Paul McCartney, Paul Rodgers, Rod Stewart, Robert Plant…Sam Cooke! No one has ever said Rod Stewart sang like Sam Cooke, but he did! So why the fuck do people say I sound like Rod Stewart?! I never get credit for doing anything original. People always say 'Oh, he sounds like a poor man's Rod Stewart.' Fuck them, man!"

Don't Say No bassman Clarke also remembers the time he served as "introductor" between Squier and a certain old friend of his. "25 or 30 years later, I'd worked with Roger Daltrey several times and the Who were playing at Jones Beach Theater on Long Island, and Robert Plant was opening for the Who – with his band. And I asked Roger, 'Can you get me some VIP passes? Because I want to bring Billy.' I remember introducing Billy to Robert Plant backstage. And Robert was like, 'Oh, finally…we meet!' And Billy made some reference to, "A lot of times, I remember when that album came out…'Is that Robert Plant's solo album or something'?" But he never made a conscious effort to do that. He just didn't. That's just Billy's voice, God bless him."

However, there were moments in interviews back in the day where it was hard to take Squier seriously when he'd conveniently fail to mention Zeppelin's influence on *Don't Say No* – such as the time in *Circus Magazine* when he was quoted as saying, "The whole British music scene of the mid-sixties had a pretty profound effect on me. It started with the Stones, the Who, the Kinks, and the Beatles. British rock n' roll became the gospel for American kids like me."

But there are also gentlemen like Eddie Trunk, who doesn't hear much sonic correlation between the Zeps and William Haislip Squier. "Billy Squier is a favorite artist of mine. And I always heard people talk about *Don't Say No* sounding like Led Zeppelin. And I've got to be honest with you, I never felt that. And I *still* don't. I could be wrong – obviously, everybody's got their opinion. But I never listened to *Don't Say No* and thought, 'Oh, this sounds just like Led Zeppelin.' I think a lot of people thought that in the tone of Billy's voice, maybe. And yes, Bobby's drumming. But still to this day, I just didn't feel that was so 'Zeppelin-y'."

Although Chouinard's Bonham-like drumming style could be heard on subsequent Squier albums (especially the title track of 1982's *Emotions in Motion*), the quality of the material on *Don't Say No* was never to be matched again – with each subsequent album selling less and less…until Squier would take a sabbatical in the early '90s (and sadly, Chouinard passing away on March 8, 1997 at the age of 43).

Looking back today, Clarke still has fond memories of Chouinard. "I miss him so much. He was brilliant. One of the nicest guys. Bobby was absolutely wonderful – he just had too many demons in his closet. Billy asked me to come

35 LED CLONES

back [for 1989's *Hear & Now*] and I did. And Bobby was having a real tough time with his personal life and it was affecting his playing. And Billy called me up and asked me, 'What do you think about using another drummer?' And we used Anton Fig. But it wasn't the same. And when we just did a new track, Billy was trying to go for something, and I said, 'You never had to do that in the past with Bobby, did you?' There was a hole were Bobby was. And he didn't get the credit because his demons took him out of the limelight too much to keep him out there and on top."

And it turns out that it was not only Chouinard who successfully recreated the gonzo drum sound of Bonzo around this time. As previously mentioned, Kiss' Peter Criss somehow "pulled a Chouinard" *before* Chouinard on side four of *Alive II*. But with Criss having exited the band in 1980 and the group seemingly stuck in a rut of three artistic decisions that saw their fanbase dwindle considerably Stateside (first a disco tune, then a pop record, followed by an indulgent concept album), it seemed like "the heavy Kiss" had been permanently retired. But they finally back came to their senses just in the nick of time with their 1982 offering, *Creatures of the Night*, which put Criss' replacement, Eric Carr, front and center. And whereas Criss came more from a Gene Krupa/Charlie Watts style of drumming, Carr was all about John Henry Bonham – and it was never more on display than with his drumming on Kiss' tenth studio album overall.

"I think Eric was a big Led Zeppelin fan, and he was always into the whole 'John Bonham thing'," Anthrax drummer Charlie Benante recalled in the 2011 book, *The Eric Carr Story*. "He played Ludwig, as well. I just think he captured what he wanted to on that record. The drums sound so big and large. If you listen to the fourth side of *Alive II*, the drum sounds on that record were great. They had some big tones on that record. And I think on *Creatures of the Night*, they captured that sound as well. It just fit the songs. So I thought that was a great Kiss record." To sample what Benante is talking about, be sure to concentrate on the drumming within such tunes as the album-opening title track, plus "I Love It Loud," and the album-closing "War Machine."

And just how did Carr go about creating such a gloriously Bonzo drum sound? It appears as though mic'ing had a lot to do with it during the album's recording at two different studios (Record Plant and Record One, both located in Los Angeles), and also, the input of producer Michael James Jackson – who co-produced the disc alongside longtime Kiss-sters, Gene Simmons and Paul Stanley. And within the same *Eric Carr Story* book, Jackson gave the lowdown on creating Carr's now-famous *Creatures* drum sound.

"We ran two studios at the same time, in the same building, and we'd go back and forth between the two of them. We put Eric in a separate room by himself. There was a big focus on trying to get as close as possible...not to the exact sound of John Bonham, but we tried to get some of the character of Bonham's sound. You can't ever duplicate what anybody else has done, because it's not just the echo, it's not just the environment, it's not the ambience – it's also the sound of the drums, the way they're hit. There's so many factors involved, [like] the humidity in the room. All those factors are involved in what the overall ambience is and sound is. But there was a real determination to try and create a sound that really had a character to it, that was along those same lines."

"So Eric was put in a separate room – not even a booth [but] a separate room – and was close-mic'd and distant-mic'd. We had spent a lot of time – we might have

37 LED CLONES

spent a couple days – trying to really work and find the sound, specifically around the drums. Because on that record, the drums have a character to them. That is what gives that record an identity. Eric was way into it, because it was his 'glory moment.' It was when all the focus was on Eric. He was willing to do whatever it took to achieve that particular thing, and also, was very focused on his playing. I always appreciated that he really cared about exactly what he did and how he was going to sound."

Jackson then explained how the final ingredient turned out to be the album's mixer, who would soon go on to become one of the music industry's top go-to knob turner. "And then later, that record was mixed by Bob Clearmountain. It was made very clear to Bob that the particular overall character of the drum sound was a key element in the record. So when he mixed it, he added some of the echo that the Power Station became very famous for. There was an elevator shaft there, that he had put a microphone down. He could send the signal into the elevator shaft, which would resonate, and the mic would bring that back. So some of that is also mixed into the drum sound on *Creatures*. Clearmountain did a great job, because one of the hallmarks of Clearmountain in those days was he had the unique ability to get more low end onto a record that would translate over the radio. A lot of engineers can put it on a record, but you never hear it on the radio. Bob had a methodology where he could really sculpt that in, in a way that if the record got played on the radio, you could hear that low-end character very clearly."

Unfortunately, a decision was made after *Creatures* – probably due to the fact that it did not sell as well as hoped (although it has gone on to become one of the band's most beloved albums amongst fans) – that Kiss would shift gears with each resulting album they issued in the '80s, and seemingly follow trends of whichever rock band was en vogue at the time. So, despite the same production team in place for its follow-up, 1983's *Lick It Up*, the bionic Bonzo power of the drums on *Creatures* was nowhere to be found…and would never be heard again on a Kiss studio recording. Sadly, Carr would pass away on November 24, 1991, at the age of 41.

When asked if he heard a "Bonzo similarity" between the drummers who kept the beat on *Don't Say No* and *Creatures of the Night*, Eddie Trunk was willing to answer the question…and even introduced another name to the discussion. "I think Bobby Chouinard was probably a little bit more 'Zeppelin-y' – because Bobby played single kick. Another guy that comes to mind is Leonard Haze from Y&T. The same thing – big, big single kick drum, really using that kick drum foot and putting those accents in, which was such a John Bonham thing."

"I think with Eric Carr, sonically the drums got really big, but he was coming from a little different place. Any drummer loves Bonham. But I think with Eric Carr, he was replacing a guy – Peter Criss. Peter Criss played a single kick and came from a swing background. And Eric Carr just wanted to be *his own guy* – he was coming in with a much bigger kit, bringing in double bass which Kiss never had before that. So, I think his drive was a little different than just, 'I'm going to be a Bonham guy.' He wanted to blaze his own path with Kiss and show he was doing something different than the guy he was replacing. But any drummer is going to obviously give the tip of the hat to Bonham. But I think with Eric Carr, it was more about the sound. With somebody like Bobby Chouinard in Billy Squier, it was more about channeling what Bonham did and more of the approach that Bonham had."

In the wake of *Don't Say No* and *Creatures of the*

39 LED CLONES

Night, a few other bands arrived on the scene that were unashamed to display their love of Led, including a band that "Fast" Eddie Clarke launched shortly after getting the boot from Motörhead, called Fastway (a band which was originally going to be comprised of Clarke and ex-UFO bassist Pete Way…hence, their name). And their best-known album, 1983's self-titled offering, certainly contained some Zep replications, including "All I Need Is Your Love," "Heft!", and their best known tune, the rock radio/MTV hit "Say What You Will."

Another similar outfit that arrived at the same time was Vandenberg – which was led by Dutch guitarist Adrian Vandenberg (what was up with the seemingly never-ending amount of metal bands in the '80s named after the last name of a certain band member?). And like the aforementioned Fastway, scored a lone rock radio/MTV hit at the time, "Burning Heart," which seemed to be somewhat modeled after a slow-building Zeppelin epic. But another connection between Fastway and Vandenberg with Zeppelin was the fact that both their singers, Dave King and Bert Heerink, respectively, borrowed from Plant's look from the '70s – particularly, flowing long hair (red in the case of King, blonde in the case of Heerink). However, Adrian Vandenberg's association with one of the most renowned "Led Clone" bands of all-time was just a few short years away. Stay tuned…

Also, who could forget Zebra – led by singer/guitarist Randy Jackson (no, not the "*American Idol* Randy Jackson")? Hailing from Long Island by way of New Orleans, the band certainly got Zeppy on their self-titled debut from 1983. Produced by Jack Douglas, the album was often tagged in the press at the time as the "fastest selling debut album in Atlantic history" – after it peaked at #29 on the *Billboard 200* and earned gold certification. But wasn't

Atlantic the same label that released Zeppelin's debut way back when? Jackson once explained exactly what the heck this bold claim meant.

"Now, a debut album for Atlantic meant that the band couldn't have put out an album before, and nobody in the band could have been on a record before. I don't know how many Led Zeppelin sold when their first record came out, but Jimmy Page had been with the Yardbirds, so he had been on record. They didn't count them. Anybody who had a career in recording was not counted, but this was a debut album and everybody on the record was their debut. And yes, it was the fastest selling, which meant that obviously we promoted ourselves into being one of the biggest bar bands in the world, and people wanted the record. I think the record may still stand for a new debut artist, because I can't imagine selling that many records that quick – it was only like, ten days we sold almost 100,000 records."

But unlike say, Squier, Fastway, or Vandenberg, Zebra also had an unmistakable proggy side to them. So, while their biggest hit, "Tell Me What You Want," featured Jackson doing his best high-pitched Plant impersonation behind the mic, he would often choose to strum his six-string rather than pluck a rockin' riff a la Page. Additionally, Jackson opted not to go the "teenager in heat" route concerning song lyrics he penned for Zebra – unlike Plant during his Zep daze.

"If you look back at Led Zeppelin in particular, a lot of what they did, they got together and they were working and grabbing anything they could to make songs," Jackson once pointed out. "And a lot of what Robert Plant did in the very beginning was just take some of the old blues song lyrics and twist them a little bit to make them his own. But it wasn't really *his* lyric. So what he liked singing would come out later – you'd hear it in stuff like 'The Rain Song.' But the

41 LED CLONES

early stuff was all raw sex. It never crossed my mind to do anything like that. Back then, we played those songs – or songs like them – but yeah, I wanted the stuff to kind of last and be a little more mature. Lyrically, I was more influenced by the Moody Blues than anybody else."

Lastly, one shouldn't assume that lyrics to a tune like "Tell Me What You Want" were autobiographical, according to Jackson. "A lot of people say, 'Oh, you must have had a tough time, y'know, tough relationship.' But it really wasn't that. I would just look at other friends of mine mainly, and write their stories. Y'know, try to empathize with them and that was where a lot of these songs came from – 'One More Chance,' 'Take Your Fingers from My Hair.' All the 'love gone wrong songs' – 'Tell Me What You Want.' They were really not so much about me but about people I knew."

And while Zebra was unable to sustain their early success, the band remains in business to this day, with Jackson never being ashamed to expose his love for Zeppelin's music – as evidenced by singing lead for performances dubbed "The Music of Led Zeppelin," in which he sings their classic tunes accompanied by an orchestra.

Also around this era, aforementioned Canadian rockers Triumph issued one of their best-selling albums, *Allied Forces*, which also spawned the classic tune "Fight the Good Fight," and according to Rik Emmett, was indeed full of Led. "A song like 'Fight the Good Fight' would never even have come into existence if there hadn't been Led Zeppelin. We never would have pushed our arrangements in the directions we did, if we hadn't been modeled on being a Zep cover band in the bars during our early days – never would have incorporated the 'float' and the heavy punch, never imagined the harmonic landscape, the guitar tones. It was the breeding ground for all of that, for us."

Despite countless hard rock and heavy metal bands stylistically visiting the land of Led during this time, Plant was not a fan of AOR (album oriented rock). And rather, was enjoying listening to entirely non-metal hit makers of the day. "I think it's…comfortable," he once said in the early '80s. "Too comfortable. And boring. That's why the Human League are good. That's why the English Beat are good, you know? That's why the Stray Cats are good, why Heaven 17 are OK."

And why did Plant list those artists in particular? "Because they all sound different. Yazoo [Yaz in America] are excellent – I mean, they just split up, right? – but her voice [Alison Moyet], combined with those modern techniques…the b-side of their latest single is incredible, it's brilliant. It's a masterpiece of modern technology with a voice that's singing. It's not deadpan, not a real boring, semi-suicidal vocal – which, well, there's a lot of that about, you know? It's got all those incredible swirls and the brassy, cutting edge of the blues voice."

In fact, Plant seemed to want to distance himself away from the metal bands that were rocking arenas in the '80s. Including one time when he went on a rant after spotting a poster of Judas Priest in his then-manager's office. "If I'm responsible for this in any way, then I am really, really embarrassed. It's so orderly and preconceived and bleuurghh. Hard rock, heavy metal these days is just saying 'Come and buy me. I'm in league with the Devil – but only in this picture because after that I'm going to be quite nice and one day I'm going to grow up and be the manager of a pop group,' or whatever. Zeppelin was never saying that."

Perhaps one of the more surprising instances of a band embracing their inner Zeppelin was when one of their direct competitors of the late '60s/early '70s reunited in 1984 – Deep Purple. Issuing their first LP with their classic "Mach

43 LED CLONES

II" line-up in over ten years, *Perfect Strangers*, there was no mistaking which band they sounded strangely oh-so-similar to on the album's quite cinematic and "Kashmir"-like title track. But unlike most of the other artists in this chapter that rode the Zep train for all it was worth, Purple was only a passenger for this tune. So, no harm, no foul. And when I once had the opportunity to interview Purple singer Ian Gillan, I couldn't help but ask him about the track and its creation.

"We had been apart for a while, so 'Perfect Strangers' is a contradiction in terms, like an oxymoron. That was pretty much how we described it – there was a lot of suspicion and worry and nervousness about getting together again and having a reunion, and when we all sat around in the basement of this old house in Vermont, there was a log fire and three feet of snow outside. We had a couple of beers, and nobody started playing. Then, Paicey [Ian Paice] started tapping away and people started grooving, and a little shuffle came along. In five minutes everyone had a smile on their face. So, 'Perfect Strangers' was how we were before, and 'Perfect Strangers' are how we are afterwards – with two opposite meanings to the phrase."

It was also around this time that the surviving Zeppelin members decided to continue their musical careers…albeit, separately. Jimmy Page was the first one to release a post-Zep offering, with the soundtrack to the 1982 film *Death Wish II*. An absolutely *awful* film starring Charles Bronson…but, with a surprisingly good soundtrack (certainly one of Page's best post-Zep offerings) – with several Zep-like numbers in the vein of their last two albums, such as "Who's to Blame." In fact, Plant enjoyed Page's soundtrack so much that he selected it as one of three "desert island albums" in 1985 (along with Eddie Cochran's *Greatest Hits* and an untitled offering from This Mortal Coil) during a chat with the radio station Q107. Which, while an interesting listen, he may have gone a bit overboard – I'm quite certain *Death Wish II* is not his most played album on Spotify in 2024.

As previously mentioned, Page would then offer up two recordings as part of a short-lived collaboration with Paul Rodgers, The Firm (which also included future Blue Murder bassist Tony Franklin and future AC/DC drummer Chris Slade), 1985's self-titled debut and 1986's *Mean Business*, and scoring a hit single/video with "Radioactive," before sailing off into the sunset. The last release by Page in the '80s would be a solo album, *Outrider*, which featured guest spots by both Plant and John Bonham's son, Jason, while its supporting tour saw Page boldly dip into Zep's back catalogue and perform some classics.

But the first Zepper to launch a proper solo career was Plant. His solo debut, 1982's *Pictures at Eleven*, is, his best, but his sophomore effort, 1983's *The Principle of Moments*, contained his best solo song, "Big Log," for which a popular MTV video was filmed (which sounded/looked like something straight out of a David Lynch film). And the clip left quite an impression on Def Leppard singer, Joe Elliott, as he once explained:

"People don't seem to ever mention it, but I thought 'Big Log' by Robert Plant was a phenomenal video. This was Robert Plant going out on his own. Now, he'd already done a solo record in '82, and this must have been his second album by then. He was all over America in '83, just as much as a band like us or Quiet Riot. But I liked the Plant one, because it was him on his own. It was all about him. He didn't have the, 'Oh, I've got to get shots of the drummer!' It doesn't matter who the drummer is on a Robert Plant record. You don't have to do that 'balancing act' that you do with a band, where a guitarist goes, 'I should be on when it's a solo'

45 LED CLONES

and all this bullshit."

But it appeared as though Plant had had enough with Zeppelin's trademark hard rock (going so far as revisiting his early rock n' roll foots with the Honeydrippers, and scoring hits with covers of "Rockin' at Midnight" and "Sea of Love"), and even refused to perform a single stinking note of any Zep tune during his first few solo tours. "I love the numbers, but I ain't gonna play Zeppelin songs without Zeppelin," he was quoted as saying in 1982.

However, with each subsequent Plant solo release, the quality took increasingly further dips, and most of his '80s albums are now very dated sounding in the sonic department. Particularly, 1985's *Shaken 'n' Stirred* and 1988's *Now and Zen* – the latter of which spawned the hit "Tall Cool One" which contained a few samples of Zep riffs and Page even providing some new guitar work (a case of Plant cloning himself…or an attempt to beat the clones at their own game?). But speaking of "Tall Cool One," the piddly drum sound is quite comical – especially when he had previously played with the greatest rock drummer of all-time. Also, by '88, Plant had finally come to his senses and began sprinkling in renditions of a few Zep classics at his solo performances.

Also of note, according to Twisted Sister's larger-than-life frontman, Dee Snider, it was supposedly once suggested to Plant early in his solo career to give a listen to Twisted Sister's to-the-point song structures for his own originals! Now, before you spit out your Yoo-hoo in disbelief, it's not that far-fetched of a claim when you really think about it – especially when you take into consideration that Zeppelin never really followed a clear-cut verse-chorus-verse format within their songs.

"I remember being blown away the first time I met Plant," Snider once admitted. "And he told me that his guy he was writing with or producing him was playing him Twisted Sister, just trying to show him like, 'song structure.' Because Zeppelin never really did traditional songs. My mind was kind of blown. I was like, 'Holy shit. He was listening to my music? My hero listening to *my* music'?"

And lastly concerning the ex-Zeps solo treks, Jones' only '80s release was the synth-pop soundtrack to another stinky film, *Scream for Help*, which leads one to wonder, who was Jones' and Page's agents when it came to landing them soundtrack-writing gigs? Surely, you'd think that former members of Zeppelin would have attracted much higher quality films…but judging from these two terrible films, apparently not. Not to be a mean-spirited man, but "Boy, the solo efforts from Plant, Page and Jones in the '80s were really on par with Zeppelin's work" said no one. Ever. OK, OK, *besides* "Big Log." Which, in defense of Zeppelin, this is not uncommon for former members of a legendary rock band to issue solo albums that are far from on par when compared to the ones with their main employer (Queen and the Rolling Stones immediately come to mind).

"I don't think that they really pacified Zeppelin fans," explains Eddie Trunk about the aforementioned '80s era solo offerings. "Which may be another reason for some of the hard rock bands of the '80s kind of channeling that sound – because I think they went off on some different trips. I mean, Jimmy Page did a soundtrack and different sort of stuff. Robert Plant's music got a lot more toned down – it wasn't as bombastic, wasn't as loud, wasn't as heavy, wasn't as hard. And he certainly has continued to follow that – where he's touched on everything from bluegrass to all these different genres that he wanted to expand into. Although Robert Plant certainly got rock radio airplay and had some success, I think most of them kind of went a little different than Zeppelin and kind of changed it up – and that also opened the door a little

47 LED CLONES

bit for some of these other bands to try and fill that sound."

But undoubtedly, the most significant '80s occurrences for Zeppelin post-Bonham's passing were the two times they opted to reunite for one-off mini-performances. The first one occurring on July 13, 1985 at JFK Stadium in Philadelphia for Live Aid (a star-studded concert that raised funds for famine relief in Ethiopia), and the second on May 14, 1988 as part of Atlantic Records' 40th Anniversary Concert at Madison Square Garden in New York City. Unfortunately, both performances were simply atrocious – supposedly either due to lack of rehearsal beforehand, or, simply lack of concentration.

In fact, concerning the Live Aid performance (which saw renditions of "Rock and Roll," "Whole Lotta Love,' and "Stairway to Heaven"), it seemed like the band did as much as they could possibly do to sabotage it. Plant opted to perform the night before Live Aid at the Joe Louis Arena in Detroit as part of his *Shaken 'n' Stirred* tour – rather than giving his voice a night off before what was to be one of the top concert events of the decade. Add to it Page's guitar being out of tune, the decision to have Plant's solo band bassist, Paul Martinez, supply bass for "Stairway to Heaven" (whereas back in the good old days of Zeppelin there was no need to do so), and the biggest flub of all – having *two drummers* replace Bonham, Tony Thompson and Phil Collins.

Now of course, Thompson and Collins are exceptional drummers in their own right (the former with Chic and the Power Station, the latter with Genesis and as a solo artist), and if it was just Thompson by himself – who was a hard-hitting drummer, a la Bonzo – it may have worked out better. But instead, some genius thought it was a good idea to invite Collins to join in on the fun – despite having played earlier that day at the Wembley Stadium in

London edition of Live Aid, and learning the tunes on the flight over! Not to mention it being an extremely indulgent decision – a round-trip Concorde flight from the UK to the US around that time cost an average of $12,000, which is equivalent to $35,000 in 2024 dollars – which leads one to figure that it would have been more beneficial to just donate the cost of the plane ticket to those in need.

Three years after the performance, Plant voiced his displeasure. "We rehearsed with Tony Thompson and then Phil Collins came on his plane and we virtually ruined the whole thing because we sounded so awful. I was hoarse and couldn't sing and Page was out of tune and couldn't hear his guitar." However, he did find at least one redeeming quality. "But on the other hand it was a wondrous thing because it was a wing and a prayer gone wrong again – it was so much like a lot of Led Zeppelin gigs."

Looking back on Zep's Live Aid debacle a decade later, Plant remained not pleased. "Live Aid was such a fucking atrocity for us. It made us look like loonies. The whole idea of playing 'Stairway to Heaven' with two drummers while Duran Duran cried on the side of the stage – there was something really quite surreal about that. I thought, 'Are we supposed to be Sinatra? Is this 'My Way'?"

"I didn't think much of it," Rik Emmett admitted about Zeppelin's lackluster performance at Live Aid. "But then again, I never thought much of live, multi-act shows that were switching up. Often to me, the moments that work the best would be someone that was working completely against type. So for example, Sting comes out and sings a song with an acoustic guitar or one electric, and has no band at all. And you go, '*Whoa*. That was gutsy. That was taking a chance'."

Def Leppard's Joe Elliott also once shared his candid thoughts with me about this controversial performance. "It's

49 LED CLONES

not really fair to tell, because the sound was so bad. When they started playing 'Rock and Roll,' the distortion coming out of either Phil Collins' or Tony Thompson's high-hat, that just ruined it all. Robert's voice is cracking a bit, Pagey I think was all smacked up. It's a hard one to call. I think most people were just glad they were on the same stage. It wasn't as bad as everybody made it out to be. Most of it was technical problems."

And while it was indeed "gutsy" of Zep to reunite for Live Aid, it's still unconscionable that Plant, Page, and Jones didn't have the wherewithal to realize they should have put more effort (and certainly, rehearsal) into making it a stronger performance. Emmett sees it both ways – "The general public may see something like that and go, 'Oh...they didn't think that one through. That was kind of self-indulgent'."

"But I think from *their* perspective, they see it as, 'Well, this is a one-off. We're just going to do it and we'll see how it flies. We'll do it for fun. We're not going to do it imagining that we're going to take over the world.' But the problem for that is if you're Led Zeppelin and you took over the world at a certain point in time – and you *ruled* the world – it's like, if you come back and you don't really rule the world with what you do, you look like an emperor without clothes. It's like, 'Oh. That's disappointing. That's heartbreaking.'"

It also turns out that around this time the surviving Ledders congregated with Thompson to jam and pen some new material – which ultimately, failed to cross the finish line. As Plant later recounted, "Jimmy had to change the battery on his wah-wah pedal every one and a half songs. And I said, 'I'm going home.' Jonesy said, 'Why?' 'Because I can't put up with this.' 'But you lived with it before.' I said, 'Look, man, I don't need the money. I'm off'." Interestingly, he described the two or three original songs they worked on as sounding "Like David Byrne meets Hüsker Dü" – which would have been in sharp contrast to all the metal bands that were digging for Led at the time.

Despite the writing session ultimately falling flat, Plant/Page/Jones still agreed to take part in the Atlantic Records' 40th Anniversary Concert three years after Live Aid, and apparently took this one a bit more seriously – as evidenced by video footage of the group actually *rehearsing* before the performance and the wise decision to have just *one* drummer on hand, Jason Bonham. However, it was still a sloppy/forgettable performance. The setlist proved to be a bit more interesting than Live Aid however, as the quartet slogged through a mini-set consisting of "Kashmir," "Heartbreaker," "Whole Lotta Love," "Misty Mountain Hop," and the obligatory "Stairway to Heaven."

By this stage, it was quite clear that Page's guitar skills had seemingly largely deteriorated. For those who think I may be just a tad too severe in my assessment, compare how inspired and fiery his playing was in his unaccompanied solo in "Heartbreaker" from the live Led LP, *How the West Was Won,* recorded in 1972 (from the 2:07 to 4:59 mark to be precise, which even includes a brief bit of Johann Sebastian Bach's "Bourrée in E minor") compared to how he was playing at Live Aid or Atlantic Records' 40th Anniversary Concert. *I rest my case.*

Interestingly, although now largely considered a dud, Kerrang! reviewer Derek Oliver gushed about the performance shortly thereafter – as if he had just seen Zep at their '73 peak. "They looked the coolest I've seen them for years; Plant hair long and lean as a puma, John Paul Jones trapped behind his keyboards like a mad professor, Jimmy Page looking much thinner and remarkably slinky, and finally, behind the drum kit, Jason Bonham whacking the

51 LED CLONES

drums so hard n' heavy that I thought they might splinter and turn to dust."

But Oliver didn't just stop there, when he continued to kiss their keisters by gushing, "If the Live Aid show was a relative disappointment then this performance certainly made up for everything that went wrong on that warm summer evening." And while he may have been laying it on a bit thick, he was indeed spot-on considering at least one assessment, when discussing "Kashmir": "Fuck Kingdom Come, this was the biggest, hardest riff I've ever heard."

However, perhaps the humdinger of all the over-the-top praise was when he said, "They were in tip-top riotous form and the crowd couldn't believe their ears." In Oliver's defense, he was probably writing this immediately after witnessing the affair in person and caught up in the moment, without the aid of watching and then re-watching – as most Zep fans have over the years.

"The common thought on both of them [Live Aid and Atlantic Records' 40th Anniversary Concert] is neither of them lived up to the billing for various reasons – that both of them could have been better," recalls Eddie Trunk. "Whether it was rushed, or the drummer wasn't right, and 'It wasn't Zeppelin without John Bonham.' You heard all of that."

Trunk also recalls a mindset that he and quite a few other younger Zep fans had concerning their heroes (who were then in or about to enter their forties)...which from today's standpoint, proves a bit comical. "It's funny too when you think of it now, because now we routinely have bands that are playing well into their 70s and 80s. But I do remember then that it was even thought of as like, 'Oh...Zeppelin's old. They're too old – they should probably stop.' And of course, they weren't *nearly* as old as by comparison what we're seeing now."

Despite Zeppelin's lackluster Live Aid and Atlantic

40th performances (the group was – rightfully – so dissatisfied with the former that they supposedly forbid it from being included as part of the four-DVD set, simply entitled *Live Aid*, in 2004), it seemed to kick of a whole new wave of "Led Zeppelin mania" in the US. In fact, Zeppelin seemed to be just as popular – possibly even more so – than when they were still in business. The proof? MTV having special "Led Zeppelin Weekends" and airing *The Song Remains the Same* concert film quite often, radio stations heavily spinning Zeppelin tunes and even having "Get the Led Out" type specials where all you'd hear was Zeppelin for an extended period (and the emergence of "classic rock radio" around this time also helped), magazine coverage, a popular unauthorized book *Hammer of the Gods* by Stephen Davis, rumors swirling about if the surviving members would reunite or not, etc.

Additionally, Led Zeppelin was undoubtedly one of the best-marketed rock bands when it came to merchandising throughout the '80s – if you recall the amount of t-shirts that had the band's logo or some other design related to the band that were regularly sported by John Bender types in your high school. Heck, *I* even remember donning not one but *two* Led Zep patches on my beloved and extremely comfortable denim jacket during my freshman year of high school: the "Stairway to Heaven" design seen within the gatefold of *Zep IV*, and also a green and sparkly "Knebworth '79" one…despite living in New York – some 3,449 miles from Knebworth.

The result of all of this "Zeppelin oversaturation"? The mid to late '80s going down as probably *the peak* Led Clones period.

CHAPTER IV
THE '80s (PART TWO)

The first band we'll discuss from "phase two" of the '80s will be Great White. By their look and production of their records, the group – who were led by singer Jack Russell and guitarist Mark Kendall at the time – were a hair metal band. But as evidenced by the vocals of Russell, he was a dead ringer for Plant – particularly on such tunes as "Rock Me" and "Save Your Love" off their 1987 album, *Once Bitten*. And as Russell once admitted, "To be honest, myself and Mark have always held the belief dear that if we couldn't make it on the strength of the music, well…a band like Zeppelin had the music, and the music was all that mattered."

And the leading UK metal mag at the time, *Kerrang!*, was going gaga over the band, when they gave them a four out of five review for *Once Bitten*, and writer Malcom Dome gushed, "Jack's voice is a natural one. He may not be a great singer, but he sure as hell is a wonderful vocalist, a storyteller, narrator. He feels the lyrics, fuels 'em and fires 'em with enthusiasm and momentum, imagination, sensitivity and fury. He bends and brushes the words at will, always sounding as if he's singing 'em for the first time and is on a glorious personal voyage of discovery. A true star."

Dome also included the following nugget in the review, which further exemplified why Brit mags such as *Kerrang!* were a cut above their US competition…I mean, who else but *Kerrang!* would go out of their way to offer up such thoughtful, image-inducing prose about a bloody Great White tune!

"So, what of the numbers themselves? The flagship is current single 'Rock Me' (already a chart hit in the US). In a way, this is the antithesis of the 'hit 45.' It builds slowly, almost lazily, arching its back only as the chorus comes into 'sight.' There's a languorous, almost sedate atmosphere here, but underpinning the entire number is a smoke-filled bar at four in the morning as the last drops are drained from the night and the bottle is allowed to slowly slip across the counter. Bass lines (from the new-departed Lorne Black) pummel out a streetcar named Emily Sleaze, Kendall's guitar firmly picks its way through the shards of broken bottles and empty dreams as Russell's voice slides to the floor in a slither of despair. And then…bursts of flame, the lights are thrown into gear and the entire band fluoresces into the infectious chorus."

But backing up a bit, a large contributor to Great White's sound and direction was a chap by the name of Alan Niven, who managed the group from 1982 through 1995 (and also managed a little band by the name of *Guns N' Roses* from 1986 through 1991) – in addition to co-writing and co-producing many of Great White's albums. And as he explained to me in 2024, helped mold the group early on – and also, recognized Russell's vocal familiarity to Plant.

"In the early days, Great White were a wannabe 'Van Priest.' And those are different vocal influences. But it was obvious to me from the get-go that Jack had a vocal tone that had a very similar quality to Robert Plant. And it got to the point that after the debut record [1984's self-titled] that didn't do what it was supposed to do – which, was not a big surprise, because it *wasn't* a very good record – I decided that we had to do something to move away from the misplaced ambitions of the past and settle into the character and qualities of Great White. 'How do you sound? What can you play?' And it was obvious to me that Mark Kendall had a tremendous affinity for putting feeling into a blues feel."

"We'd been in the studio recording demos, and between takes, Kendall would be playing a blues lick. And I'm sitting in the control room, going, 'It's right in front of

55 LED CLONES

you Niv, what you should be doing with this band.' So, for me, my intention was to steer them back towards the early '70s. To steer them back to British blues rock. And in that respect, bands like Ten Years After and Savoy Brown were influences. And in terms of Led Zeppelin being an influence, you had to be *really* careful in how you wrote and arranged the song – because you didn't want to end up sounding like a band that was trying to mimic Led Zeppelin. Of which there were what, two or three bands that came along in the '80s that were mimics. You had to be careful."

"There was one night I sat Jack and Mark down, and thought, *'I need to play them this record.'* So, I start playing them this record, and they're looking at each other, they're looking at me, and they're scratching their heads. Eventually, Jack finally comes out and says, 'Niv, why is this old black man trying to play Led Zeppelin?' And the record was Willie Dixon's *I Am the Blues* [which includes the original versions of 'I Can't Quit You, Baby' and 'You Shook Me']. Especially Jack loved Led Zeppelin, but it was amazing to me that they didn't know who Willie Dixon was."

And while "Rock Me" was singled out at the time as sounding quite Led-like, Niven disagreed. "'Rock Me' had its own tones and sound, but it had a particular arrangement and approach to the dynamic. So, I felt what we did in terms of the arrangement and how we utilize dynamics within the song was particular. It wasn't a mirror of something that somebody else had done before. We were working in a blues idiom. And when you're working in a blues idiom, it's really hard to sound fresh and unique. But I think we managed it with that song. I think that still sounds fresh."

Around the same time as the success of "Rock Me," Russell discussed the band's sound. And as expected, Zeppelin was mentioned. "I think it's more heart and soul than anything else. It goes back to what I was saying earlier as far as not trying to write hit songs, just trying to write what's in here. Everyone's writing formula rock, like Bon Jovi did this, we saw somebody else do that – fuck it man! Let's just go back to the roots. Let's go back to what got our dicks hard when we learned how to rock n' roll, try to remember what it's all about; why I'm singing in a rock band is because of bands like Aerosmith and Zeppelin."

Russell also made reference to simply "the blues" being an influence – another route many Zep disciples seemed to take in interviews around this time, rather than stating the obvious. "It all comes down to the fucking blues. Like, 'What do you have?' The blues! I've got some bimbo in my right ear, the landlord yelling in my left, the manager bawling at the front and some record company guy fucking me in the ass from behind, so I've the fucking blues."

But undoubtedly, the greatest evidence that Great White was under a deep Zep trance was when they performed a spot-on version of "Since I've Been Loving You" on an MTV *Live at the Ritz* concert special in 1988 (while Russell sported a tie-dyed Zep shirt!), plus "Babe I'm Gonna Leave You" (particularly Russell's carbon copy Plant vocals) for an appearance on MTV's *Unplugged* in 1990. And perhaps most glaring of all, when they issued the album *Great Zeppelin: A Tribute to Led Zeppelin* in 1998, which included fourteen faithful readings of Zep classics. And let's not forget a sorta follow-up in 2021, *Great Zeppelin II: A Tribute to Led Zeppelin,* albeit credited to Jack Russell's Great White (as was the case with several '80s hair metallists, there were *two different* versions of the band in business in later years).

"Jack loved singing Zeppelin," recalls Niven. "In February of '88, they were filmed at the Ritz in New York, and we decided that we allowed 'Since I've Been Loving You' – which is one of the most traditional forms of a blues

57 LED CLONES

song that Zeppelin recorded. And they *nailed* it. And then of course, we were asked to do *Unplugged* – this was the first session of *Unplugged* being recorded in LA. We were asked to do it two days before we recorded. So, it wasn't like we had a lot of prep time, or had a lot of thought going into this. But I'm driving Jack over to A&M Studios in my Jag, and I play him a song, and I go, 'Do you think we can pull this off?' And he looks at me and says, 'Well...let's rug jam it when we get there and see if we can put it together.' Literally, Jack and I went into the green room, sat the band down, rug jammed the song, they went out and did one rehearsal without audience, and then came out and played it. And that was 'Babe I'm Gonna Leave You.'"

"Which, it would have been – believe it or not – the very first *Unplugged* record released, had I not said, 'No.' Would I have made the same decision today? I don't know. But at the time, I thought, 'This is supposed to be special for a particular circumstance. You get to see the performance and hear the song if you're watching MTV. I only have a two-track, I can't remix any of this. I'm not sure that this is in the correct spirit of what we're doing – to release it.' But for me, personally, the validity of doing those two songs came from the fact that when I was a nipper, I saw Zeppelin three times. And I was disappointed every time – because it might just have been the inebriation was getting the better of the band, and the performances were not stellar. In fact, the third time, I left before the end of the gig because I was *so* disappointed."

"So, for me, the validity in recording these songs and having them filmed was, 'I know *my* band can play these. I know *my* band can pull them off. I know that *my* band can probably do them even better than the original guys – because they were always drunk all the time.' And they went out there and nailed this stuff. It's kind of funny when you watch the clip of 'Babe I'm Gonna Leave You' from *Unplugged*, because if you watch Kendall's right hand, he has got the most chronic case of the shakes. He is *so* nervous about not fucking up, and you watch his right hand – you can see it shaking all the time. But they pulled it off. And it was utterly a valid performance of a couple of great songs. When it got to after I was no longer working with the band, Jack did one, two, three…maybe *20* tribute records of recording Zeppelin songs. That to me was, 'No. That's *not* valid.' That boils down to, 'I can't write great songs and I need some money…so I'll sing some Zeppelin songs. And I like singing Zeppelin songs.' It didn't really have a profound validity to me."

And when I asked Great White's former manager the question, "Which other Great White songs were influenced by Led Zeppelin?", he wound up flipping the question. "That's a difficult one. Don't forget, you're talking to the main writer in the band. As part of the process, you're looking for a phrase, you're looking for a lick that speaks to you. And then, you form it into a rudimentary arrangement, and then you start to second guess – 'Is this something that I've heard before? Am I just paraphrasing something that I heard a long time ago?' And you spend a certain amount of time reassuring yourself that what you are working on was not something that somebody is going to walk up to you in three months' time and go, 'That's so-and-so's song!' And that was a major part of forming songs."

"So, in the compositional aspect of Great White, I worked really hard to make sure that I wasn't doing something that was a mimic of Zeppelin. I think it's fair to say that in the lyrical content, we were a fair bit away from Zeppelin. But the flip question is, 'Which Great White song would Led Zeppelin cover? And, could they do it…and could they be convincing doing it?' I think 'Maybe Someday'

59 LED CLONES

[off 1992's *Psycho City*] is a song that I can hear Plant really nailing and delivering. But it's an interesting thing, because the entire music is built brick upon brick."

Lastly, Niven shared a story he once heard that took place sometime during Great White's late '80s peak. "There was a moment at a party in Brazil, where Joe Elliott was talking with Robert Plant, and he said, 'Hey, Robert. Have you heard that person in Great White? He sounds a bit like you do, doesn't he?' And Plant looked at him and said, *'He sounds more like me than I do.'*"

Around the same time as Great White's ascent, another hair metal band was also picking a scrap or two off the Zeppelin carcass – Cinderella. Admittedly, the group – led by singer/guitarist Tom Keifer – had much more in common musically (and visually) with Aerosmith and the Rolling Stones. But, they did have a few Zep detours, such as the title track from their sophomore effort, 1988's *Long Cold Winter,* which sounds like it's not exactly a million miles away from the land of "Since I've Been Loving You."

And Keifer has given several nods in the press to the Led lads over the years, including the time he admitted, "I grew up with rock music of the late '60s and the mid '70s. I learned to play guitar and write music from a band like Led Zeppelin – they were a big inspiration for me. Led Zeppelin had so many different flavors in their soup – take for example a song like 'Over the Hills and Far Away,' it had an acoustic Celtic vibe then it kicks into the heavy-duty electric rock part then back down. It's that kind of contrast and blending of musical styles into a rock album that I've always loved. Those are my influences and I try to keep that alive as I write and make records."

Also, when I spoke with Keifer once upon a time for *Classic Rock* about his "10 Records That Changed My Life," one of his selections was *Physical Graffiti.* "I remember getting *Physical Graffiti* for Christmas, putting it on, and hearing 'The Rover,' 'In My Time of Dying,' 'Kashmir'...that record was just mind-blowing. I don't think there's a rock musician from my generation that wouldn't say that *Physical Graffiti* wasn't a major record for them. Very inventive record."

Up next, let's discuss Whitesnake, shall we? Truth be told, unlike the majority of the other '80s Zep scholars, Whitesnake really only knelt at the Led alter one time. But boy, was it a doozy – the song "Still of the Night." Originally hitting the big time in the early '70s as the replacement for Ian Gillan in Deep Purple (who along with the Rolling Stones were probably Zeppelin's closest competition at the time), singer David Coverdale launched Whitesnake shortly after Purple's initial split in 1976. And on the strength of such albums as 1980's *Ready an' Willing*, 1981's *Come an' Get It*, and 1982's *Saints & Sinners*, the band was suddenly one of the top hard rock/heavy metal bands in Europe. But...US chart success eluded them.

Coverdale seemed to meet his perfect foil when ex-Thin Lizzy guitarist John Sykes swooped in – in time for 1984's *Slide It In*, which managed to just scrape the top-40 on the *Billboard 200*. So it didn't take a leather-clad Einstein to figure that the band was on the cusp of a true global breakthrough with what was to be their seventh studio effort overall. And while Sykes would co-write every song on the subsequent album with Coverdale (except for two re-recordings of earlier W. Snake tunes, "Crying in the Rain" and the mega-hit "Here I Go Again"), by the time of the album's release on March 23, 1987 – going simply by the title *Whitesnake* – Sykes was surprisingly already given his walking papers.

"You see, I got fired from Whitesnake," Sykes explained not long after his exit. "The thing was we went and

61 LED CLONES

wrote the material together and it was in France, and I went over with [Coverdale] – just me and him alone – and we wrote the songs for the album. After that, we flew out to Los Angeles because we moved management, and [management] was out here and the record company was out here, so we both come out here, and found Aynsley Dunbar – because Cozy [Powell] had just left. We went up and started recording the album in Vancouver at Little Mountain, and we laid the backing tracks down and stuff, and he went in to start doing vocals. And he had a problem doing the vocals, and we all wondered what was going to happen. Then we decided it was probably the weather that was causing his throat not to work, so we came back to Los Angeles and tried it down here, and then we flew out to the Bahamas after that, and it still wasn't happening. This went on for a couple of years."

"Finally, he went in and had an operation on his throat and sang the album, and said to me, 'Look, go to England and do your guitar. Finish off the guitar, do your guitar solos.' 'Cause you lay them down after the vocals. And I went to England and did that. Halfway through guitars, I found out that Mike Stone the producer had been fired, and Neil [Murray] and Aynsley had been fired. And I thought, 'This is strange.' So then I found out that they wanted the tapes back on that weekend, which was a Friday, and this was like Wednesday. I kept phoning him up and he wouldn't return any phone calls or anything. He never even told us we were fired, he just sort of ignored us all and took the album and ran."

Years later, Coverdale gave his side of the story concerning why things didn't work out between him and Sykes. "As you know, things went squirrely between us, which was unfortunate. But John was and is an incredible talent. Our musical chemistry was great, but it didn't work personally. The truth of the matter is no matter how incredible of an album that we made together, we were unable to connect as people. You can hear that there was creative magic in that relationship, but it stopped the moment we put the mics and instruments down. John was critical to that record and a superb live player. But there were many important aspects of things that were not there. It wasn't meant to be. With John, things just exploded. I think rock bottom would have been when he tried to fire me from my own band. As you can imagine, that didn't go over very well." [Laughs]

But it was during the writing sessions for the album that the aforementioned "Still of the Night" was penned. "We were jamming on ideas," Coverdale once recalled. "I had this riff for a while I'd found in my mother's attic on an old cassette. I wanted a kind of 'Jailhouse Rock,' which is one of my favorite rock songs ever – my introduction to Elvis Presley, courtesy of my Auntie Sylvia. So, I played these things to John and he took the riff to you know, *cosmic levels*. And the rest is history." And while a bit of a tune by Elvis the Pelvis may have served as the guitar riff's initial inspiration, by the time it was laid down in the studio, it sounded 100% Zeppelin derived – seeming to be an amalgamation of "Black Dog" (the riff, the call and response between the vocals and riff, etc.) and "Whole Lotta Love"…with a dash of "Kashmir" (particularly the middle breakdown) sprinkled on top.

In fact, another noted *Kerrang!* writer at the time, Dante Bonutto, had the cajones to ask Coverdale point blank around the time of the album's release, "But, but, baby, baby, baby isn't it just that bit too close to Zeppelin to still be Whitesnake?" Coverdale's reply was sly – as he utilized the aforementioned "we share the same influences" easy-way-out response. "Yes, but then Zeppelin were very *Beck-Ola*

63 LED CLONES

and *Truth* (two Jeff Beck Group albums from the late sixties). Don't forget I come that same era, and besides, who else is doing that sort of stuff now?"

"The thing is, we sat down and said, 'What are we going to do in the middle section?' I wanted a real wild thing for John to fly on, but nothing was working. So I said, 'Bugger it, let's do atmospherics!' We were rehearsing the idea and Aynsley started tapping around and I went, 'Is that a bit close?' But then I thought, 'Who gives a damn?!' It's exploring, taking it further, there's cellos coming in and stuff."

Another time not long after the album's release, Coverdale opted to toss up a bit of word salad concerning 'snake's sudden approximation of Zep. "Actually, I guess it's quite a compliment to be placed in a class like that," he said. "But I don't know how accurate the comparison is. People shouldn't forget that I worked in Deep Purple for a number of years, so my pedigree in hard rock is quite strong. I understand that bands like Whitesnake, Purple and Led Zeppelin all play a solid, powerful brand of rock, but I don't think we're coming from the same place musically. I don't mean that literally, because I do believe there is something to being a British rock n' roll musician. There is a special quality that I haven't found anywhere else in the world."

By the time a music video was filmed for "Still of the Night," Coverdale was the only geezer from the song's recording left in attendance, as Sykes was replaced by not one but *two* shredders – ex-Vandenberg's Adrian Vandenberg and ex-Dio's Vivian Campbell (with Ozzy's former rhythm section, bassist Rudy Sarzo and drummer Tommy Aldridge, also doing battle). And the video proved to be incredibly popular with still-major-tastemakers MTV – which prominently featured one of the era's top music video vixens, Tawny Kitaen (who was briefly married to

Coverdale), as well as Vandenberg incomprehensibly ripping off Jimmy Page's violin bow gimmick!

Years later, Coverdale seemed to express some grief concerning allowing Vandenberg to wield the bow in the video. "Adrian brought the bow and he said, 'What about this?' And I'm going, 'Oh, fookin' hell, I don't know, that's just a bit fookin'...', y'know." And everybody's going, 'Why not?' It was one of those 'Why nots.' Aw, fook it. It's something one tends to regret later." Not to pass the buck, but in defense of Vandenberg's not-exactly-wise decision, there were other metal shredders of the '80s that also opted to glide a bow across their guitar strings a la Page in "Dazed and Confused" – namely, Vinnie Vincent during his stint with Kiss and Carlos Cavazo with Quiet Riot.

And although Whitesnake did succeed in claiming an enormous new audience Stateside with their "Zeppelin pastiche," it left older fans with a case of the blahs. Including Anthrax drummer Charlie Benante. "I used to really enjoy certain Whitesnake songs – especially the album before *Slide It In* [1982's *Saints & Sinners*]...but I do like *Slide It In*, too. But I don't understand how most people didn't see this as a Zeppelin copy band. And then when I heard 'Still of the Night,' I was like, 'This is fucking 'Whole Lotta Love'!"

But as mentioned before, "SotN" was really the only brazen Zep maneuver from Coverdale and company on their '87 offering. All their other hit tunes off the album were either of the then-thriving hair metal variety ("Here I Go Again" and "Give Me All Your Love") or power ballad heaven ("Is This Love"). But still, "Still of the Night" was hard to swallow for some. Including Mr. Plant and Mr. Page – the former going as far as amusingly referring to David Coverdale as "David Cover-version" in the press at the time.

"I spent so much time pretending I was the singer with Led Zeppelin and looking at David Coverdale and

65 LED CLONES

wondering where I was," Plant stated around the time Whitesnake was at peak popularity Stateside. "I thought, 'What a wanker, I could do that.' In fact, I *do* do that. That's me. I want my money back. And when I find him I shall get my money back! But then again, you've gotta smile and say, 'Good old David, I thought he was really Paul Rodgers.' But he's not, he's me. Next year, he'll be Paul Rodgers."

Page on the other hand, found some of Whitesnake's clear Zep maneuvers to be a bit entertaining – for all the wrong reasons. "To tell you the truth, when I saw Whitesnake's video and there's a part where the guy starts playing with a bow, I actually fell around laughing…literally. I was sitting on the bed watching it, and I promise you, I fell on the ground laughing. I mean, if he can be that cheap, that's alright. Because I've heard it – in the song they don't even use the bow, it's all in that part. That's how silly it can become, that someone would actually do that and be prompted into standing there with a bow. I find it a bit cheap."

And Plant would later expand on what really got his goat concerning Coverdale. "I know the guy. I've spent nights occasionally talking to him in the past. I find him a good man, but I feel that his integrity is now questionable. If Whitesnake was a real young band who had just seen *The Song Remains the Same* and decided, 'OK, this is it, let's imitate them,' I could understand it. There was a time, years ago, that I tried to mimic Elvis Presley. That's quite acceptable. But David Coverdale's nearly my age. He is of my genre, even if he was in a lot of substandard groups. Really, you shouldn't do it to your own gang, you know."

"When I aped somebody, they were so remote, it was like they were millions of miles away. When somebody you know, somebody you've bought a drink for, suddenly comes out and looks like you and is you, you start wondering, 'Well, maybe it wasn't me who went out with that girl in Dallas, maybe it was him!' Of course, he's only been doing this recently. Before that, he was Paul Rodgers. Sure, I'll probably bring the matter up next time I see him. But I shan't even bother to say anything. I'll let my right foot, which has scored a hundred goals, do the talking."

As a result of being on the receiving end of all the bashing, Coverdale eventually seemed to reach his breaking point, when he was once quoted as saying, "There's certainly no love lost between myself and Robert. I wouldn't send him cat food if he was starving." However, fast-forward to 2013, and Coverdale claimed to have asked a mutual acquaintance (Jimmy Page!) to pass along an olive branch to the Golden God. "My last words to Jimmy in London were: 'I'd love to buy Robert a drink.' I said, 'When you speak to him, offer my sincere regrets for any negative things I've ever said, which were mostly defensive.'" Whether or not both are now exchanging Christmas cards is unknown.

One last observation concerning Blanco Serpiente – courtesy of Eddie Trunk, in which he questions if the group's brief merge into the Zep turning lane was not entirely Coverdale's doing. "I think also when *1987* [the UK title of the group's self-titled release] rolled around, David decided to just rev everything up and changed the band and brought in John Sykes on guitar. And then Sykes comes in with these gargantuan riffs that were Zeppelin-esque, Coverdale just adapted to that. But if you really know the history of Coverdale and what he was doing prior – it was very much his own thing. And also, very much rooted in the blues."

Also the same year that Whitesnake's self-titled offering slithered out, one of the '80s seemingly completely forgotten Led Clones appeared – a bloke by the name of Michael White, who fronted a group called Michael White & the White (I know, certainly not the most *imaginative*

67 LED CLONES

band name ever) issued an album simply titled...*Michael White*. It's producer? None other than Mack, who was behind the board for Billy Squier's *Don't Say No* and *Emotions in Motion* (in addition to most of Queen's '80s LP's).

There is no debating that Mr. White's vocals are absolutely a carbon copy of Plant's (hell, judging by the album cover photo...he even *looked* like the bugger!). But for the most part, it sounds more like Plant's early '80s solo albums than prime '70s Zeppelin. But there is one exception – the tune "Psychometry" is one of the most glaring Zep facsimiles ever, from top to bottom. If you're not familiar with the tune, be sure to look it up – you'll be left flummoxed. And a reason why it sounds this way is because White had apparently assembled a Led Clones all-star band to back him up on the album – Billy Squier keyboardist Alan St. John and drummer Bobby Chouinard, plus Moxy drummer Danny Bilan!

And there is a humorous tale concerning White, told by bassist Greg Chaisson (who was a member of a Zep-influenced band, Badlands, which we will soon discuss in chapter seven). "Ray [Gillen] was at a bar in London, and he sees a guy at the bar and he thinks it's Robert Plant. The guy is dressed like Plant, has hair like Plant, standing like Plant. So, Ray is going to go say hi to him. He walks up to the guy, and as he gets closer, he realizes, it's not Robert Plant...*it was this guy, Michael White!*"

Could artists sound any more "Zep derivative" than Whitesnake on "Still of the Night" or Michael White on "Psychometry"? Somehow, someway, the seemingly impossible *did* happen – in 1988.

CHAPTER V
THE '80s (PART THREE)

And now, dear readers, we have arrived at a crucial point in the book where we will now discuss/analyze the *biggest* "Led Clone" of them all…Kingdom Come. As mentioned in this book's intro, throughout the course of rock history, there are instances where certain bands are shameless rip-offs of others. And certainly at the top of the list would have to be Kingdom Come's love affair with the music of Led Zeppelin – as no band before or after has been so thorough in their Zeppelin obsession.

Led by German singer Lenny Wolf (whose previous claim to fame was fronting the obscure outfit Stone Fury), Kingdom Come was rounded out by guitarist Danny Stag, guitarist/keyboardist Rick Steier, bassist Johnny B. Frank, and drummer James Kottak at the time of their 1988 self-titled debut. And as Wolf once explained, the songs came fast and furious after his split from Stone Fury. "I immediately went to the music stores and started buying lots of instruments and a four-track tape recorder to make some demos. Then I locked myself away for three months and wrote 50 songs. I couldn't stop them coming out, hardly any of them took me longer than half a day or so to write."

When I spoke with Kottak for *BraveWords* in 2018, he recalled how he landed the gig. "Funny enough, I auditioned with Lenny, and there were probably 50/60 drummers. And Lenny and I hit it off – we clicked right from the minute we met. And then along comes Danny, Johnny, and Rick, and the next thing you know, Derek Shulman from Polygram came to a rehearsal, listened to three songs, and said, 'Let's go make an album.' The next thing you know, we're in Vancouver with Bob Rock – from Mötley Crüe and Metallica. This was kind of his first big solo venture, because

69 LED CLONES

he was Bruce Fairbairn's right-hand guy. We did that album, and honestly, without sounding corny or dorky, it was really magic."

Issued on February 29, 1988, majorly backed by Polygram Records, and as Kottak just mentioned, co-produced by Wolf and a pre-Metallica Bob Rock, Kingdom Come's self-titled debut was a sizeable hit straight away – peaking at #12 on the *Billboard 200,* going gold in both the US and Canada, and helping the band secure a spot on the hottest US rock tour that summer, the Monsters of Rock (which saw KC open a bill that also featured Metallica, Dokken, Scorpions, and headliners Van Halen).

And another major contributor to the success of the "Get It On" single (which peaked at #4 on Billboard's Album Rock Tracks Chart) was MTV's support of its video – which Kottak later shared his memories of filming. "We went to the warehouse to do it, and it was this massive set-up – trees, like we were out in a forest. It was unbelievable. It cost like, $110,000! I was going, 'What?!' That's what videos cost to do back then. It was a surreal experience. And that day, we took a break somewhere during the shooting, and we had a convertible – a Cadillac – and we went for a cruise down Sunset, and that was the first time we heard 'Get It On' on the radio – on KLOS. We freaked out. That was a banner day."

But seemingly from the get-go, the band came under fire from the press and from fellow rockers – quickly becoming one of the top rock bands "you love to hate." And looking back, Kingdom Come can be filed in the same category with the likes of Shania Twain, Garth Brooks, Vanilla Ice, Nickelback, and Kid Rock. And what category may that be? It's the mysterious – but apparently quite lucrative – "artists who have sold a bazillion albums but I don't know a single person who owns one" classification.

THE '80s (PART THREE)

In a review issued around the time of the album's release, *Kerrang!* scribe Mick Wall exclaimed, "What we've got here isn't so much *Kingdom Come I* as *Led Zeppelin XI*. 'That good?' I can hear you asking yourself. Yeah. And that bad...meaning...everything about Kingdom Come – the guitars, the drums, the riffs, the lyrics, the voice (Oh my God, the voice!) sounds exactly like Led Zeppelin! As in EXACTLY THE DODDMAN SAME!!" However, Wall admitted in the same review as to being baffled concerning his true feelings – "As for me, I like it a lot. But then I was always fan of Zep's. Which is why I will never love it. Confused? You will be. As for Bonzo, he would have puked." And then perhaps most shockingly of all...giving the album a 4 out of 5 possible review!

Elsewhere, renowned/outspoken rock critic Robert Christgau would also give the LP a surprisingly high rating of a "B," but admitting "I'm not curious enough to ascertain which Zep songs provide which hook riffs, but that doesn't mean I can't lay back and enjoy a musical force as musical form." But keep in mind, this is the same punter who gave quite a few now-widely considered classic rock albums *extremely* mediocre ratings, including "awarding" Pink Floyd's *Dark Side of the Moon* a B, Metallica's *Master of Puppets* a B-, Guns N' Roses' *Appetite for Destruction* a B-, Van Halen's self-titled debut a C, and Black Sabbath's *Paranoid* a C-. So, in other words, was Kingdom Come's self-titled debut on par – if not superior – to these other true rock n' roll masterworks? I don't think I even have to continue this discussion/explanation to prove my point, do I? Good, I knew I didn't have to.

Even Jimmy Page offered his two cents on the sudden hottest topic within rock. During a chat with *Kerrang!* in June of '88, writer Mick Wall inquired, "I wanted to ask you about that, I mean, have you heard this

71 LED CLONES

band Kingdom Come yet?" Page then replied, "Kingdom Clone?" The former Zep guitarist would also add, "Um, I've heard the album a couple of times. I must admit there are a few moments when there were sort of ghosts walking out – the ghost of myself so many years back, you know?"

Judging from Page's "Kingdom Clone" quote and the earlier observation concerning Plant's "David Coverversion" insult, the former Zep members seemingly never backed down from lobbing a good old fashioned insult upon other rockers. But this was nothing new, as John Paul Jones offered some simply *scorching* remarks upon Jethro Tull's Ian Anderson and Deep Purple/Rainbow's Ritchie Blackmore during a chat with journalist Steve Rosen back in 1977:

"Ian [Anderson] is a pain in the ass. We toured with Jethro Dull [sic] once and I think he probably spoke three words to Jimmy or I at any one time. The band was nice but he was such a funny fucker. His music bores the pants off meit's [sic] awful. Page came up with the greatest line about them. He had a title for a live album when Jethro was playing in Los Angeles: *Bore 'Em at the Forum*. [Ritchie] Blackmore is another guy I don't like. He was supposed to have been a big session man but he must have done demos because he was never a regular session man. I'm getting out all my pet hates."

But back to Kingdom Come, seemingly, just about every time Wolf conversed with a journalist in 1988, the resulting article seemed to come off more as an interrogation rather than an interview. But to the singer's credit, he always offered an answer…despite it not continually being a completely honest one. Such as the time he stated, "This isn't some cheap rip-off and we didn't go out of our way to sound like Led Zeppelin, all we sound like is Kingdom Come. It's up to the kids to decide whether they like it or not. Five years from now I bet they'll actually accuse other bands of sounding like us."

And while the last sentence of that previous quote just might be the most ludicrous of the entire book, the singer did make at least one valid observation at the time (which we will further explore later in the book): "Led Zeppelin copied a lot of the blues musicians, people like John Lee Hooker and Willie Dixon. All I'm trying to say is that every musician is influenced by somebody, it's a very natural and normal process. Normal, that is, so long as you don't steal parts."

Guitarist Stag also got into the act of passing the buck concerning why KC sounded so much like LZ. "Every rock drummer in the world wants to sound like John Bonham but it just so happens that James can pull it off. Put him together with Lenny, who's a great blues singer, and me, who's a blues-influenced guitar player, and what have you got? You got a band that sounds like Led Zeppelin. I don't try to sound like Jimmy Page; he's not even one of my influences."

And through it all, Wolf was adamant that the similarity between the two was all one big happy accident. "You start writing a song, play a little lick and all of a sudden, oops! You've created something that already exists. It's just your subconscious transferring the lick and you don't remember it at the time but then you realize it later. It's happened to me twice, but no, I didn't listen to Zeppelin when I wrote those songs. It's all my own stuff."

And that was the whole problem with Kingdom Come. If you take a close listen to their lead-off single/video, "Get It On," you can actually pinpoint which Zeppelin tunes or bits they swiped, such as the opening riff sounding like an amalgamation of "Black Dog" and "Heartbreaker" and the music underneath the verse being a snatching of "Kashmir." And let's not forget the very Bonham-like drum break that

73 LED CLONES

signals the conclusion of the song. But probably the most obvious Zep fleecing was in Wolf's spot-on Plant vocal impersonation throughout (and to add insult to injury, while the rest of the band dressed like your average hair metal band of the day, Wolf would dress similar to Plant – tight jeans, unbuttoned shirt, bare chest exposed, etc. – as evidenced by the pic in the middle of this very book).

But truth be told, the entirety of their debut was not all Zep, as heard by such decidedly hair metal fare as "The Shuffle," "Now Forever After," and "Shout It Out." But there were certainly additional Zep moments – Wolf's carbon copy of Plant on the ballad "What Love Can Be," Kottak's Bonzo bashing that opens "17," etc.

Ultimately, Kingdom Come's time in the sun would be extremely fleeting. "The first album was what it was," Kottak explained, years later. "And then, this other little band called Guns N' Roses came along. When Guns N' Roses exploded in the summer of 1988, it was kind of like, 'Kingdom who?' Guns N' Roses just swept everybody under the rug. And then fast-forward to our second album, *In Your Face*, by then, the musical climate had changed, and the labels were trying to sign anybody that was like, sleaze rock or whatever you want to call Guns N' Roses. But it was a phenomenon. There hadn't been anything like that – other than Nirvana – since, that I can recall. They changed the landscape. Kingdom Come was always 'the odd band out.' We were kind of like, hard rock with a bluesy edge – at a time when hair metal was ruling. There were so many great hair metal bands – if you want to call it that. We were the odd band out."

While speaking to former G n' R manager Alan Niven for this book, I had the opportunity to read him the aforementioned quote from Kottak (who sadly passed away on January 9, 2024 at the age of 61) to get his feedback. He replied: "I feel a bit sad for him – because he obviously feels that something out of his control maybe hampered or took away his future. I would also – if I had a scotch or two and was drinking with him – look across the table and say, 'You made your own bed. Everybody thought you were 'Zeppelin lite' instead of 'Kingdom Come strong.' So, you basically ran your course on one album – where everyone went, 'Wow. This is like Zeppelin. This is not cool, because Zeppelin is great.' But on the other hand, did you ever really find out who Kingdom Come was?'"

"And the other thing is yeah, G n' R exploded, we all got singed eyebrows. And record companies are *so* ordinary. Y'know, 'This works…let's try it again. Oh, it worked again? Let's try it again.' Wherever they think there is a line of least resistance and that something is easy to market in the wake of something else, they will do it. One of the things that I was proud of, of Great White, was we never made the same record twice. And that was because I ensured Capitol left us alone – so, we could 'be of the moment.' And not be doing what Def Leppard does, for example – which is make the same record over and over again."

"And let me tell you, I think Def Leppard are my all-time favorite 'boy band.' But that comes down to some incredible production work and a lot of aural sugar. I laughed when they came out with the song 'Pour Some Sugar on Me,' because that's what Mutt Lange did with a Def Leppard record – he'd pour a whole bunch of sonic sugar on you. It would be delightful to listen to, but at the end of the day, if you're only eating dessert, you kind of go, 'I'm feeling undernourished. What does this band actually stand for – in terms of intelligence and soul? What are they really talking about? Is there anything here that moves my intellect?' And there isn't. But, on the other hand, they sound so good. *But it's just sugar.* Listening to Def Leppard is like getting a really rich dessert for appetizer, and a really rich dessert for the main course, and oh, by the way, here comes the pudding – another really rich dessert."

An while we're on the topic of Guns N' Roses, I couldn't resist but asking Niven if the band was influenced by Zeppelin at all. His response was as follows: "Izzy [Stradlin] was not particularly a Zeppelin fan. He was way more into the Keith Richards/Ronnie Wood mode. And Axl [Rose] spent *hours* in the shower mimicking Dan McCafferty from Nazareth – to try and sound like a real rock n' roll singer. So, you know that he was moving in a completely different direction than Plant."

"And as for Slash, of course he knows Zeppelin and is very aware of it all…but there was a moment early on, when Slash came down to the tiny office I had. We were discussing this, that, and the other, and I looked at him and said, 'What do you want to get out of this?' And he looked at me and said, 'I want to be recognizable.' Now, he wasn't talking about top hats. For him, the most important thing that he could achieve was to develop his own voicing and style, and his own way of playing – that you could recognize his playing in a piece of music if it was him. So, again, he wasn't trying to be Jimmy Page. Slash wanted to be *Slash*. So, in terms of influence, it's like anything magnetic – you're either drawn to or repelled. In the case of Great White, they were more 'drawn to.' In the case of Guns N' Roses, they were more 'repelled.'"

While it appeared as though Kingdom Come was the brunt of many a joke ever since their inception, there is no denying that they were quite popular during 1988 – with MTV and rock radio giving some serious airtime to "Get It On." And Eddie Trunk remembers this period of peak popularity for the band, as well.

"I worked in radio when Kingdom Come came out.

There were people that would call them 'Kingdom Clone' and they took shots at them. What I found interesting about Kingdom Come – even at that time – they took all this shit for being so Zeppelin-like, but 'Get It On' was a *huge* song. And radio played the hell out of it. I remember that there would be DJ's that would even goof on it or make a snide comment about it sounding so much like Zeppelin…but they were *still* playing it, and they *still* blew it up, and they *still* made it a huge record. I always found that interesting."

"Now, it was almost like, 'OK, we're going to give them this one with 'Get It On,' because it's undeniable. But then…you're not going to have a career after that.' Because then, it was 'one and done,' pretty much. But I always found that whole thing interesting about Kingdom Come, that out of the gate, they were considered just this 'poor man's Zeppelin rip-off,' but in reality, they got a ton of airplay and sold a couple million records off that thing. It sounded so good on the radio that radio could not *not* play it. I think that was a case of the music and the production and everything just connecting. And everybody was like, 'Well yeah, of course it's Zeppelin. But it's still pretty darn cool'."

And as it turned out, other sub-genres of rock also had bands that were closely examining Zeppelin in the '80s…

CHAPTER VI
THE '80s (PART FOUR)

Within the realm of alternative rock, one of the leading artists often linked in the '80s to Zep would certainly have been the Cult. However, this British band started out as a jangly sorta guitar outfit (courtesy of Billy Duffy) with Jim Morrison-esque vocals (provided by Ian Astbury) on such albums as 1984's *Dreamtime*. By 1985's *Love*, the Zep detector began buzzing – particularly on the track "Phoenix," which includes a part at the beginning that is unmistakably similar to "Dazed and Confused." "We'd already been through the post-punk/post-modern scene since 1981," recalled Astbury years later. "So it was time to transition. We were going back and discovering all the music we weren't supposed to be listening to – everything pre-1976, early Led Zeppelin records, the Doors and Blue Cheer."

However, the Cult's music sonically was still very much entrenched in '80s alt-rock terrain. But that all changed with the arrival of 1987's *Electric,* when they suddenly decided to fully embrace classic rock of the '70s – not just songwriting-wise, but also, production-wise, courtesy of a union with Rick Rubin. "The Cult had just signed with Sire Records, and we came to New York to do a photo shoot for *Rolling Stone*," the singer recalled. "We'd started recording with [producer] Steve Brown, but as soon as I heard Rick's work, I was like, 'Stop everything – let's go to New York and find this guy!'"

And found Rubin they did, who had previously worked primarily with hip-hop acts (Beastie Boys, Run-DMC, LL Cool J, etc.), and only one rock act (thrash metallists Slayer). It turns out that right off the bat, he laid down the law. "When we first met, I was a 23-year-old crazy kid," remembered the singer, during a conversation with

Rubin. "The next thing I knew, you're showing me a VHS tape of Blue Cheer doing 'Summertime Blues,' going, 'Do you want to play pussy English music – or do you want to rock?'"

And at one point during the album's creation, everyone involved seemed to fall under the spell of Zep. "There was an amazing store called Rock and Roll Heaven across the street [from Electric Lady Studios, where the album was mixed]. We'd go on a pilgrimage in there, perusing old magazines, posters, paraphernalia. They had the Led Zeppelin tree, Rick Griffin posters, obscure vinyl. It was a Holy Grail of this period we were enamored with. We'd take these artifacts back to the studio, like, 'Check out this picture of Jimmy Page in *Creem* magazine from 1975!' We even had Zoso t-shirts made up." Rubin confirmed this claim as fact: "We did! We'd also watch old videos, like this black-and-white recording of Led Zeppelin on a TV show, around the time of the first Zeppelin album."

And Rubin has always clearly credited Zeppelin's – or rather, *Page's* – production and sonic approach in the recording studio. "In the case of Led Zeppelin, Jimmy Page's production is astounding. It definitely takes it beyond what the live recording can do. In the case of Led Zeppelin, it starts as a live recording in the studio, and then he adds layers and layers of embellishment that make it a symphonic recording rooted in a live rock band recording."

One thing that is undeniable about the resulting Cult/Rubin album was that sonically, it served as a much-needed antidote to all the overly-produced rock albums of the mid-late '80s – as it was almost a precursor to the grunge bands of the early '90s. Why? Because it was a conscious return to the sound of a band playing live in a room. However, while there was at least one slight nod to Zep on the recording – the riff to "Electric Ocean" – there was

79 LED CLONES

another classic rock band they were shamelessly pilfering from…AC/DC.

For shits and giggles, the next time you are bored to tears and in desperate need of entertainment, try doing this: play the album's lead-off track, "Wild Flower." And as soon as it starts, sing the lyrics to AC/DC's "Rock n' Roll Singer" off their classic *High Voltage* LP (y'know, "My daddy was working 9 to 5, when my mama was having me…") – and you will find that it sounds like a virtual carbon copy. Elsewhere, the tune "Bad Fun" contains a bit straight from "Beating Around the Bush" in the verse, while "King Contrary Man" features a *total* Angus Young solo.

And back around the time of the album's release, Astbury opted to "pull a Lenny Wolf" rather than come clean, and played the "we share the same influences" card. "I don't think anything on that record really does sound like Led Zeppelin, or AC/DC, or the Rolling Stones. It sounds like us playing blues-based rock music. It's a very traditional kind of thing. We're more like a traditional band in the sense that our influences lie in blues-based rock music – that's what I was brought up with and that's what I'm into, and that's what we sound like. I think if we came out with an album that sounded like the Pet Shop Boys people would REALLY be pissed off with us."

But it turns out that the Cult were not done breaking off a crumb from the Led bread, as evidenced by the selection "Soul Asylum" (not to be confused with the "Runaway Train" alt-rock band) off their 1989 album, *Sonic Temple*, which contains a "Kashmir"-like guitar bit and unmistakable Bonzo bashing courtesy of session drummer Mickey Curry. Early in Guns N' Roses' career, Axl and co. opened a tour for the Cult. So, who better than their manager at the time, Alan Niven, to share his thoughts concerning if Astbury went the "Robert route" vocally at all. "I really liked

Ian as a frontman. Yes, you could say he was a little Plant-esque. But I thought his personality was a little more interesting. I thought Ian's presence had a darkness about it – that inspired curiosity. Their track, 'Sun King,' I thought was fucking brilliant – I *loved* that song. Yes, it's Zeppelin-esque…but it was *the Cult*."

Another British alt-rock outfit that was also accused of Zeppelin worship was the Mission (known as the Mission UK in the States) – probably due in part that none other than John Paul Jones produced their sophomore full-length, *Children.* But I'll be honest – listening back to the LP today, the Zep-detecto-meter barely gave off a single blip – except maybe for the beginning of the tune "Fabienne." Perhaps merely a case of rock journalists getting ants in their pants concerning sounding off the Zep-alarm at anything remotely containing a big guitar riff at the time?

Perhaps the most surprising alt-rock band that attended Zeppelin University around this time was Public Image Limited (better known as "PiL"), featuring former Sex Pistol John "Johnny Rotten" Lydon on vocals. Why was this so surprising? Because back in the '70s, the Pistols – understandably – took aim directly at "rock dinosaurs" such as Zeppelin, who had seemingly lost touch with their audience (surrounded by bodyguards, traveling via limos, living in castles, etc.), and was growing further away from their early/rawer approach. However, it was during the '80s that PiL was known to make their concert audiences dumbstruck by laying an instrumental cover of "Kashmir" on them – as a set-opener!

Lydon once explained why he opted not to "pull a Plant" like so many others at the time, and vocalize over their cover, and also, how he actually fancied a particular Zep LP. "I was supposed to run on and do the Robert Plant bit, but no, I can't." [Laughs] I mean, we'd rehearsed it, but it never,

81 LED CLONES

ever felt right to [do it]. I thought I'd be standing in someone else's shoes at that point, but it was a good homage to a band that we do love. Although, yes, I've never mentioned Zeppelin very much, *Physical Graffiti* is one of my favorite albums. The sheer terror and ferocity of it...beautiful landscaping."

And another style outside of metal that also managed to get bitten by the Zep bug was hip-hop. And in particular, the Beastie Boys, with their 1986 break-through hit, *Licensed to Ill* – where a snippet of the guitar riff to "The Ocean" magically reappeared in "She's Crafty," while Bonzo's famous drum intro to "When the Levee Breaks" was swiped for "Rhymin' & Stealin'." But it turns out that it was from a gentleman outside the band that was responsible for inserting samples of Zep tunes into their compositions – our old pal, producer Rick Rubin. "Rick definitely came from a whole AC/DC, Led Zeppelin, Long Island, like, rock background," B. Boy Michael Diamond once recalled in *The Beat* documentary. "He, pretty much...introduced it to us. Because we kinda came from punk rock...'forget about that shit'."

And as previously explained during our little discussion concerning the Cult and their album *Electric,* Rubin worked with an impressive amount of varied artists over the years, while also, always loving himself some Zeppelin. And he once took a trip down memory lane concerning his *Ill* recording. "That one was recorded over a long period of time, and I think one of the reasons it's as good as it is, is that each song really has its own life, which I don't think would've been the case had we made the whole album in two or three months. It wouldn't have had the breadth and depth that it does, especially musically."

"That was kind of two years of our lives. Not two years of our lives in the studio every day, but we'd work on

THE '80s (PART FOUR) 82

a song for a couple of days, then we might not go back in the studio for another month or six weeks, then whatever was sort of speaking to us at that moment would be the next one. So it really came together over time, with all of the influences – both of the day and the influences we'd grown up with. I'd grown up with Led Zeppelin and AC/DC and more hard rock, and they'd grown up on punk rock, and you can feel all of those influences in that record."

Just when you thought that the "Zeppelin teet" had been milked dry by decade's end, there was still a few more drops left – the most obvious being when John Bonham's son, Jason, launched a band entitled...*Bonham*. Although it would understandably be an almost impossible challenge to follow in his father's career choice – as Bonzo is widely considered the greatest rock drummer of all-time – Jason once claimed that it was shortly after his father's passing that he made up his mind to also pursue music as a career.

"I went very quiet then. I just didn't know what to do," Jason recalled once in the late '80s. "And I just went, 'Fuck this, I'm going to go out there and prove to people that the Bonham name will carry on forever.' And I want to say, 'Let's carry on the tradition. Let's put another Bonham up there with myself.' And now, I've finally got to do that with the new band, Bonham."

Prior to the launch of Bonham, Jason had been a part of two forgotten bands that managed to issue recordings that were clearly modeled after the radio-friendly rock that MTV and commercial radio was quite fond of at the time: first Airrace, and then Virginia Wolf (the latter of which landed some plum tour opening slots: Queen and the Firm). But neither band left much of an impression musically nor chart-wise. And after young Jason supplied drums for Zep's performance at the aforementioned Atlantic Records' 40th Anniversary Concert and also for Jimmy Page's *Outrider*

83 LED CLONES

tour, he finally had some empty spaces in his daily planner.

And by decade's end, Bonham decided it was finally time to get the Led out himself, with the formation of a band that was every bit a Zep copy as most of the other acts analyzed in this chapter. Featuring a particularly Plant-sounding singer, Daniel MacMaster, plus guitarist Ian Hatton and bassist/keyboardist John Smithson, the band surprisingly opted to go with a very prog-y album title and front cover photo for their 1989 debut, *The Disregard of Timekeeping*. Produced by Bob Ezrin (best known for his work with Pink Floyd, Alice Cooper, and Kiss), all of the album's eleven songs listed all four members of the band as songwriters, with Ezrin's name affixed to three of them, and even then-Yes guitarist Trevor Rabin supplying bass and backing vocals on a few tracks.

"I grew up a bit and when I wrote the material, it felt right, felt like it would work," Bonham said back in the day. "Hopefully, the timing is right. Every other band I was involved with, there was not this atmosphere and it's creating a lot of interest because it's the first time that it's my thing and I'm involved writing-wise. Even if the time is not right, we'll disregard it!"

Material-wise, it was one big Zep fest. Particularly the album's hit song/video, "Wait for You," which the drummer described as "Something I came up with during rehearsals for the Jimmy Page tour. It was instrumental, then Danny sang on it. Sure, I was dubious at first, but I'm proud of my past and if my dad's influence had not rubbed off, I'd have to be deaf! I play drums like him and I write like him. It just happens. What works, works – if it doesn't, you throw it out – but 'Wait for You' really works."

And while the track simply *reeked* of Zeppelin, the drummer did not deem his new band a copy…and even felt confident enough about his project to throw another similarly-styled outfit under the bus! "That track has the Zeppelin mystique, yes. I don't think people will knock it because it's a part of me. It's in my blood and that's the way the song came out. Then again, we're not a clone or a copy. It might remind people of Zeppelin, but they can't say, 'That's *that!* The way they said, 'Get It On' is 'Kashmir'!' Although I won't deny Led Zeppelin influenced me!"

And similarly to most Zep forgers of the decade, Bonham fell into the same trap of going with a very '80s-styled production – meaning the power of the trademark Bonzo drum sound was replaced with that now terribly-dated canon sound, and it sounded like a pristine studio creation rather than the vibe of a band playing live in a room together a la *Physical Graffiti* at its down n' dirtiest.

And what did Zeppelin themselves think of Bonham? Plant opted to make light of the situation (I guess he was saving his real vitriol in the press for Mr. Coverdale) by stating, "How do I feel about the singer sounding like me? It's good fun, really. And I'm going to get some rawkers [royalties?] out of him…or else I shall remove a testicle."

Plant also decided to take the high road when discussing his thoughts about the music contained on *The Disregard of Timekeeping*. But also, issued a warning. "When you asked me about what Jason's record sounds like, it sounds like it's part of the current idiom of music. It fits nicely. It's played very, very well. There's a couple of really great songs on it. But Jason's got to make sure that now that he's established his head above water, and he knows who he is and what he's doing, he's just got to make sure he doesn't go back underwater. He's got to be *Jason Bonham* – that's a lot to be. To call your group 'Bonham' is a heavy thing to do – because his dad was Bonham. Not him. He's the kid, so he's got to really bring it home now."

Jason himself also discussed the risky decision of

85 LED CLONES

titling the band after his famous surname. "It's pretty tough as well to call the band Bonham. But I'm proud of the fact that I'm a Bonham, and that's why if anyone says it sounds a little Zeppelin in places, fine, I'm very proud of that too. But it's not a cloud or anything like that. Everything in my kingdom is mine."

Did young Jason heed Plant's advice and keep his head above water/making the wave that he can? Well, he was able to keep the Bonham band afloat for one more album, 1992's *Mad Hatter*, before letting it sink to the bottom of the ocean, and focusing on other projects (often Zeppelin-related, which we will discuss in detail later).

"The song 'Wait for You,' that absolutely *was* Zeppelin sounding," confesses Eddie Trunk. "And the singer, Daniel MacMaster, he looked and sounded the part. *Big time.* That one was a little bit eyebrow raising, because that could have been looked at two different ways – here is a band that sounded so much like Zeppelin, but who had the son of a Zeppelin member in it on drums. And was named after it! So, in my opinion, they could almost be given a pass, because if anyone is going to have the right to do this, it should be the offspring of a member of Zeppelin."

"But then the naysayers would be like, 'Why the hell isn't the guy just blazing his own path? He should be doing his own thing. Why is he capitalizing on his father?' But that one was one where the sound, production, and the look – especially in lead singer – was very, very Zeppelin. And again, another case where like Kingdom Come, it was 'one and done.' It was like, one big song and MTV play, but there was no follow-up to that at all."

"I think people kind of gravitate towards the novelty initially, and they hook onto it. But then afterwards, it's almost like an immediate backlash – because it is *so* similar to Zeppelin." But at least there's a happy ending to the story

– Jason did eventually carve out his niche as an in-demand hired gun, playing with the likes of Foreigner, Black Country Communion, and Sammy Hagar and the Circle, among others.

Another new act launched in 1989 was Blue Murder – which signaled the return of John Sykes after his unceremonious sacking from Whitesnake on the cusp of their massive commercial success. Teamed with former Firm bassist Tony Franklin and former Rod Stewart (among many other artists) drummer Carmine Appice, the band issued a self-titled LP produced by Bob Rock, which although didn't do much chart-wise – peaking at a paltry #69 in the US and #45 in the UK – it did seem to satisfy the needs of the rock and metal press at the time.

Listening back to the album today, the trio does indeed tip their collective cap to Zep at times. For instance, there's no denying the goliath drum sound and groove featured throughout "Valley of the Kings" is similar to "Kashmir." But as evidenced by many an interview and article, according to Carmine Appice, he is supposedly responsible for birthing "Bonzo bashing." Additionally, the opening drum part of the song "Blue Murder" is a reproduction of "Fool in the Rain" (aka "the Purdie Shuffle"), while "Ptolemy" also contains a Zep-like groove.

"I never realized what a great drummer Carmine is until I actually played with him," Sykes admitted around the time of the album's release. "He has the great Bonham feel, with that lazy snare, but he has all these intricate jazz feels and fills underneath that. He plays heavy funk really well."

Sykes also name-checked Zeppelin, as well, when admitting, "When I was younger there were all these masterful bands around, real professionals like Deep Purple, Led Zeppelin, the Who, Bad Company, Free, the list is endless!" But to his credit, Sykes never shamelessly copy

87 LED CLONES

and pasted Zeppelin riffs in his new project, which, he had seemingly done in "Still of the Night." "I drew from absolutely everything that I've ever done musically to make this record. I wanted the freedom to experiment with the songs, to do something that entailed more than the usual 'verse/chorus/verse/chorus/bridge/solo/chorus/outro' kind of thing. I didn't want to follow the usual boring route, because I've become so tired of the usual mundane crap that's around these days."

The singer/guitarist also made a conscious effort to try and move away from the style of mainstream rock that was popular at the time – "I want to show that there's a lot more to rock than leather-studded cod-pieces. What I've tried to capture on the record is a really heavy funky groove with the 120 beats per minute, relaxed tempo that gets people moving. If you can get the groove that gets people moving then you are halfway there." However, Rock's production did not reflect this, as it is certainly of the "'80s dated variety," when heard today.

Also at the time, *Kerrang!* writer Howard Johnson praised Sykes as "A man who eschews all the bogus rock star bullshit for sheer quality. It's an ethos that seems to be returning to rock n' roll with bands such as Blue Murder, Badlands, and the Cult." However, Mr. Johnson's theory would soon flounder, when a video for the Blue Murder tune "Jelly Roll" (which Johnson would also describe as having a "superb *Led Zeppelin II* sound," which I would dare to disagree with, but anyway…) would be issued shortly thereafter. In the inadvertently humorous clip, Mr. Sykes channel's Mr. Plant's "Sex God' guise – in an unforgettable scene that features him ripping off his white tank top…while caught in a rain storm!

Years after the fact, Sykes remained quite chuffed concerning Blue Murder's debut – despite its underperformance chart-wise. "It might have been a bit too heavy. That one has almost become like a cult classic. It's like a record that you really like and then still like it ten years later. It doesn't sort of get old and wear out on you. It still stands the test of time. I definitely had a lot of angst in me at that time."

One last point concerning the B. Murderers – courtesy of long-time admirer Eddie Trunk, who similarly to his feelings about Billy Squier's *Don't Say No*, didn't hear much Zep in the Sykes-led band. "Gosh, I love John Sykes and Blue Murder, but I don't get the sense that Blue Murder was blatantly going after a Zeppelin vibe. Blue Murder was more produced, it was bigger sounding. I never really put that together. I mean, you can draw the line from *anything* to Zeppelin if you really wanted to – because they were so influentially huge on such a massive amount of rock."

"But I never really got the sense that Blue Murder was coming from that. And when you look at the guitar in Blue Murder, Sykes didn't play at all like Jimmy Page. When you look at the drums, Carmine will be the first to tell you that he influenced Bonham – so you can't really make that comparison. And Tony Franklin played a fretless bass – which John Paul Jones did not." Despite an impressive amount of press coverage and a few spins on MTV, Blue Murder was not long for this world – Franklin and Appice would jump ship after the debut, with Sykes soldiering on for just one more album, *Nothin' But Trouble*, in 1993.

By this point in the '80s, it was hard not to experience some "Zep burnout" (which I even suffered a bit from), after being bombarded non-stop musically and by media coverage. Plus, of course, seemingly a new Led Clone arriving each month. As it turns out, even a member of Zeppelin could understand if others were becoming critical of his former band. "I can't blame anybody for hating Led

89 LED CLONES

Zeppelin," Plant once admitted in '88. "If you absolutely hated 'Stairway to Heaven,' nobody can blame you for that because it was, um…so pompous."

And with all that being said, I now bring you to the last chapter in which we will explore the '80s…

PHOTOGRAPHS

Led Zeppelin
1977
Photos by Christopher Lee Helton

Robert Plant
1977
Photo by Christopher Lee Helton

Robert Plant
1985
Photos by Christopher Lee Helton

Robert Plant
1985
Photos by Christopher Lee Helton

Jimmy Page
1985 (top) and 1986 (bottom)
Photos by Christopher Lee Helton

Jimmy Page
1986
Photos by Christopher Lee Helton

The Firm
1986
Photos by Christopher Lee Helton

Rush
1980
Photo by Bill O'Leary/Timeless Concert Images

Ann Wilson (Heart)
1993
Photo by Christopher Lee Helton

Aerosmith
1984

Triumph
1982
Photos by Christopher Lee Helton

Van Halen
1984 with Roth (top) and 1988 with Hagar (bottom)
Photos by Christopher Lee Helton

Billy Squier
1984
Photo by Christopher Lee Helton

Bonus Billy!
1984
Photos by Christopher Lee Helton

Def Leppard
1983

Steve Clark (Def Leppard)
1987
Photos by Christopher Lee Helton

Virginia Wolf (Jason Bonham on far left)
1986

Great White
1994
Photos by Christopher Lee Helton

John Sykes (Whitesnake/Blue Murder)
2008
Photo by Wikimedia Commons

Adrian Vandenberg (Whitesnake/Vandenberg)
1984
Photo by Bill O'Leary/Timeless Concert Images

David Coverdale (Whitesnake)
1980
Photo by Bill O'Leary/Timeless Concert Images

Jimmy Page
1986
Photo by Christopher Lee Helton

Robert Plant
1985
Photo by Christopher Lee Helton

Lenny Wolf (Kingdom Come)
1988
Photo by Christopher Lee Helton

Danny Stag (Kingdom Come)
1988
Photo by Christopher Lee Helton

Four drummers who enjoyed bashing a la Bonham:
Bobby Chouinard and Eric Carr…

...and James Kottak and Alex Van Halen
Photos on both pages by Christopher Lee Helton

Robert Plant
1985
Photo by Christopher Lee Helton

Jimmy Page
1985
Photo by Christopher Lee Helton

Soundgarden
1989

Nirvana
1989
Photos by Charles Peterson/Sub Pop

Lenny Kravitz
2004
Photo by Wikimedia Commons

Eddie Trunk (donning Billy Squier shirt)
2019
Photo by Greg Prato

Wolfmother
2011

Barack Obama, John Paul Jones, Robert Plant, Jimmy Page
2012
Photos by Wikimedia Commons

CHAPTER VII
THE '80s (PART FIVE)

Now, some readers of this book may feel I was a bit too harsh or critical about artists we've covered so far in the '80s – concerning their pirating the music of four men who came from the land of the ice and snow. But just as the '80s portion of this book comes to a close, I would like to take this opportunity to discuss a band that had a Zep influence...but got it *right* – Badlands.

Although the group had heavy (no pun intended) ties to Black Sabbath – singer Ray Gillen and drummer Eric Singer were former members of the band, while guitarist Jake E. Lee was a member of Ozzy's solo band, and bassist Greg Chaisson auditioned for Ozzy – the group did not contain one iota of Sab in their sound. But, still retained an unmistakable '70s vibe. Also admirable was their look – in which they "dressed down" and avoided many of the hair metal fashion faux pas of the day. In fact, the quartet resembled *a southern rock band* more so than *a glam rock band.*

Looking back on the album today, Chaisson explained to me just how much – or how little – of an influence Zeppelin was on Badlands. "I think the biggest influence Zeppelin-wise was Ray. Ray was a *huge* Robert Plant-ophile. Lyrically – and even with some of his vocal approach – was very influenced by Plant. As far as the writing process and the songs in general, Zeppelin would have been one of the influences that Badlands had – along with many others. And Eric, of course – you can tell on some of the stuff, is very influenced by Bonham. And I as a bass player, how can you not be influenced by John Paul Jones? I started playing in the '70s – '71, to be exact – and John Paul Jones was a 'go-to guy.' Bass players back then tended to be

91 LED CLONES

more creative and played more basslines, and were allowed to 'be off the chain' a little bit."

However, according to the bassist, the Badlander probably least influenced by Zep was Lee. When asked who were some of the guitarist's prime six-string influences, he responded, "Tommy Bolin, Frank Marino, Paul Kossoff, Jimi Hendrix, Johnny Winter, Ritchie Blackmore, and some Jeff Beck." But he did admit that "Probably any guitarist from that generation is influenced somewhat by Jimmy Page – especially Jake, if you listen to 'Winter's Call' and that whole middle section and the way that he plays that intro part, it's got a very 'Jimmy Page sort of feel' to it."

And it turns out that "Winter's Call" was not the only tune on the album that contained a slight salute to Zep – as evidenced by the track "Seasons." And Chaisson was willing to discuss both tracks. "'Winter's Call,' I wasn't there when it was written. The way that record was done was we recorded half of the record in a studio in LA, and then Atlantic pulled us out of the studio because they weren't hearing 'a hit song.' They flew Jake and Ray to New York City to write without Eric and I there – they used a bass player and drummer just while they were writing. So, when Eric and I got to New York, we were hearing 'Winter's Call' for the first time."

"'Seasons' was something that Jake had been toying with writing for Ozzy. Had he stayed in the band, maybe 'Seasons' would have been on the third Ozzy record Jake would have been on. I remember Jake was telling me to listen to what Bob Daisley had done on the demo for 'Seasons' on the bass part, because there was one particular part of the song that he wanted me to mimic Bob – not through the whole song, but just a part that might have been the bridge. There's been some talk lately that he also wrote 'Hard Driver' while he was in Ozzy. Some of these ideas he had he probably started formulating while he was in Ozzy, but as far as having a whole song that was demoed for Ozzy, I never heard anything other than 'Seasons' that was demoed while he was in Ozzy."

Another standout track was the album's lead-off single/video, "Dreams in the Dark." But according to Chaisson, Gillen's vocals on the track were not Plant-like...but were more a kin to *another* certain singer. "Ray unfortunately gets more comparisons – because of the era – to David Coverdale. And to me, I hear a little of that – especially because of 'Dreams in the Dark.' But I think that Ray was much more versatile than a lot of other singers, because Ray could sing the phonebook and it would sound good."

But the bassist clearly explained who Gillen's main vocal influence was. "Ray had clearly studied Plant at one point, because at times at rehearsal and times even live, he would hold the mic exactly like Plant or stand exactly like Plant. I think that was his go-to guy. Ray would always say, *Led Zeppelin never made a crappy song.*' We would argue about it – I'd say, 'Well...'Hot Dog.' That ain't a great song.' He'd go, 'That's a great song! Have you ever *listened* to that song'?"

"Ray was so much a fan of Zeppelin and Plant, that as far as Ray was concerned, they could have been tuning their guitars and made a song out of it, and Ray would have loved it. I think Ray liked the way [Robert Plant's] lyrics were. They had kind of a fantasy thing to them – but not something really crazy. And Ray really liked that. He definitely liked his look and vibe on stage. His vibrato."

Gillen himself was not ashamed to admit his appreciation of Plant and Zeppelin, as he was quoted shortly after the release of the album (on May 11, 1989) as saying, "Humble Pie, Free, Zeppelin – it's the music that I grew up listening to, it's in my veins, and I'm not ashamed of that fact!

93 LED CLONES

"If people come up to me and say that a certain vocal on the album sounds like David Coverdale, or another sounds like Robert Plant, then I thank them very much and say they're being way too kind! What's wrong with trying to emulate the best there is? I actually met Coverdale recently and he told me that he likes my singing. I told him the truth – that I learnt a lot of it from him – and he just smiled in a way that said he kinda knew that. Why try to take the credit away from those guys?"

The singer even pinpointed a particular Zep recording that served as an inspiration for him during the creation of Badlands' debut. "While we were recording the album I was certainly listening to *Led Zep III* a whole lot. I really love that stomping, country, downhome feel and we definitely tried for something of that feel on 'Rumblin' Train.' But there are only really three tunes that have any specific kind of Zeppelin influence, and they are 'Rumblin' Train,' 'Devil's Stomp,' and 'Winter's Call,' but even out of these tunes, 'Winter's Call' is a very old song. That was written five or six years ago!"

And while Gillen's vocals are impressive throughout Badland's debut, it seems like he somehow took it up another notch when performing live – as evidenced by two stellar performances by the band that can be viewed/heard on YouTube ("Live in California 1989" at the Shoreline Amphitheater and "Chicago 1991" at the Vic Theater). And the bassist confirmed this was no video illusion.

"He's the best singer I ever heard. I never heard Ray have a bad night. I never heard him have a bad rehearsal. He was always 'on.' The unique thing about Ray, even if we were rehearsing, writing, or doing a soundcheck, Ray would *sing*. If there was music going on, Ray would start singing and making up melody lines right from the get-go. I've never heard a singer like that. Even times when maybe we all weren't getting along, once we hit the stage, all that crap went right out the window. Ray always focused on the audience, on the band, and if we were in some kind of disagreement, you would have never been able to tell by watching us live. Ray was a professional that way."

And another thing that separated Badland's debut from most other rock bands issuing albums in 1989 – they opted for a much more in-your-face, live sound than their contemporaries (which in a roundabout way, served as a precursor for what rock records would sound like post-1991). And according to Gillen, it was no happy accident. "It took a while for our producer, Paul O'Neill, to realize what it was we wanted. The thing is, he's from the new producers, so he likes to pile those guitars up and to have a whole lot of production. Take the Blue Murder album, for example. There's so much shit on there it's amazing, which again sounds good for them, but it's not our way."

"We wanted the feel to be that of a band jamming in a garage, which resulted in a lot of yelling and screaming before Paul actually realized what kind of band we were. It took a little time for him to realize why I only wanted to do one track of vocal for most of the songs, but when I track them it tends to lose some of the rawness. We had Dave Thoener in to mix the album, and he did a lot of work with Leppard and he was absolutely raving over our approach. He said that this was exactly where he came from: one vocal, one guitar, bass, and drums."

And Chaisson corroborated Gillen's claim of "less is more" production-wise, but also explained how the producer managed to pull a fast one on the band. "The triggered part of [the drums] I think was on a snare. We didn't know about it until the record was out. And once the record was out and mastered, it became evident that that – to a certain extent – was used. But the way that they did it…I think that has to do

95 LED CLONES

more with the 'Paul O'Neill influence' that he had over the band, as far as being in the studio and getting a production credit. I think Jake wasn't even privy to it."

"Because I remember when the record came out, Eric saying, *'What happened to my snare?'* But I will give him this much credit – he did it in a way that seemed more authentic or more visceral than, for example, a 'Def Leppard drum sound.' The 'clap of thunder' thing. We kind of avoided that. When we went to the second record, that was a concern that Jake wanted to address personally – he wanted the drums to be 100% real. And on the second record, they are. Even though there probably is a little sampling on that, I thought they did a good job making it less annoying."

Despite *Badlands* being an impressively consistent listen from start to finish, it did not match the success that the band and their label, Atlantic, probably anticipated – peaking at only #57 on the *Billboard 200*. And perhaps it had something to do with the fact that the band was marketed as a "hair metal band." Which, makes you wonder if the album would have fared better if it was marketed more in line with such soon-to-be-fast-rising "retro rockers" as the Black Crowes and Lenny Kravitz?

"Yes and no," says Chaisson. "You've got to figure, that first Badlands record sold 480,000 copies or whatever it is. And probably the bulk of those people would have been people that were into the 'guitar hero thing' and Jake. And also, the people that were into the hair metal era – even though that was kind of the tail end of it. So, if we had been marketed strictly as a 'retro band,' maybe we would have lost some of that. Maybe we wouldn't. I don't know."

"I mean, you can look at a picture of Badlands and know we weren't your typical hair metal band. And I think that helped us. Had we had the right management and had we been on a label that better understood what it was we were doing and not try to make us into Skid Row, I think we would have been more successful. But in the end, it is what it is – and I'm proud of the records that we made, and I'm proud of *that* record. It's kind of taken on a life of its own for a number of reasons."

Unfortunately, the promise of Badlands' debut didn't last long – Singer would soon exit the group to join Kiss, and their sophomore effort, 1991's *Voodoo Highway*, was not as strong as its predecessor. As a result, by 1993, the band was kaput – although a set of demos for a possible third LP, entitled *Dusk*, surfaced in 1998. Sadly, any chance of a future Badlands reunion was snuffed out on December 1, 1993, when Gillen died from AIDS-related complications (at the age of 34).

Due to the likes of Whitesnake and Kingdom Come hogging the spotlight, charts, and magazines with their brand of Zep plagiarism, by the close of the '80s, a few renowned fellows seemed to relate to the famous Popeye phrase, "That's all I can stands, I can't stands no more!" – namely, Gary Moore and Ozzy Osbourne. Best known for his work with Thin Lizzy and as a solo artist, Moore has gone down as one of the greatest rock/metal guitarists of all-time – due to a playing style that could shift between metal, blues, ballads, fusion, prog, and even Celtic at times. And on his 1989 solo outing, *After the War*, Moore invited old pal Osbourne to sing a tune that took direct aim at those two particular aforementioned bands, entitled "Led Clones."

Featuring a guitar riff that was obviously modeled after vintage Page, Moore pulled no punches in the song's lyrics, including a middle part (sung by Moore, as Ozzy handled the verses) that stated, *"Got to get it on, from the still of the night, but you're gettin' it wrong, you know it ain't right."* And he was not at a loss for words while discussing the tune in the press. "'Led Clones' was written about bands

97 LED CLONES

like Kingdom Come, who take all their ideas from Led Zeppelin…who rip off bands like Led Zeppelin, and then they claim that they're totally original and they won't acknowledge the fact that they're influenced by these other people. Ozzy Osbourne sings lead on this track and there's a string section at the end, so it's got like a big '60 style kind of psychedelic section at the fade out."

Moore also dug a bit deeper concerning penning the track, and what Osbourne brought to it. "It was quite funny to do that with Ozzy and everything, and to have a bit of fun for a change. I'm sure people will see the humor in it. The riff came when I was just sitting at home one day, and I thought, 'Oh, that sounds a bit like Led Zeppelin, so I can't do it seriously or it's gonna be people saying, 'Led clone!' Then it all came together very quickly, probably in a couple of hours. It's full of stuff. Even like the string section right at the end, which is meant to sound psychedelic! I put anything in there!"

"I mean what's Ozzy doing in there? He's not like anybody else, y'know? Ozzy's got a gift. He opens his mouth and this noise comes out, and it doesn't sound like anybody else at all. And he changed some of the lyrics around: instead of singing 'I heard it on the radio…' he sings, 'I saw it on the radio, I heard it on the video,' and it was great – a classic Ozzy touch. So I kept that. It's all kind of bits and pieces. I wanted it to sound like a band in the late '60s trying to be 'creative,' almost. You know, like, 'Oh, we've been listening to a lot of Eastern music and a bit of Debussy recently' kind of thing, then they come up with something like 'Lick My Love Pump'! Real 'Spinal Tap'."

And on at least one occasion, one of the targets of "Led Clones" offered a retort. In the May 13, 1989 issue of *Kerrang!,* all five members of Kingdom Come were photographed with a black-taped "X" over their mouths, while each flipped the bird with one hand, and the other hand holding up a plate which contained one word per member, which when all added up and read left to right, said: "We are sooo sorry Gary!"

It turns out that others were amused by the "Led Clones" song…and others, not so much. Badlands' Greg Chaisson was one chap who got a kick out of it. "I'm just finishing up the Gary Moore biography [2022's *Gary Moore: The Official Biography* by Harry Shapiro], and there's a whole part in there about that. I think he's right. Gary Moore had no problem speaking his mind. And I think his main piss take was on Kingdom Come – who he called 'Kingdom Clone' – or Whitesnake as they morphed more into the Zeppelin thing. I know Gary may have been familiar with Badlands at some point, because Eric had done a tour with him, and Jake was a legitimate guitar hero of that era, as well. So, I don't think we're part of the 'Led Clones' diatribe."

However, others didn't particularly care for Moore and Osbourne's attack of the many artists who chose to go in through the out door during the '80s – such as Rik Emmett. "I think that's kind of beneath Gary. Like, why bother going there? Gary was a good enough player…somebody must have talked him into that one, I don't know."

Also, add Eddie Trunk to the camp who was not all that impressed with the "Led Clones" track. "I was a big Gary Moore fan – it's not among my favorite Gary Moore songs. I mean, it's probably just a little more of a 'message song' or a 'spoof song.' When I listen to Gary Moore, I'm cranking up 'Victims of the Future' or 'Corridors of Power.' It's not a go-to for me."

As you may have guessed by now, we are rapidly reaching the end of the '80s portion of this book. But before we put the chapter to bed, one more point needs to be made – something that many of the Zep-like (lite?) bands of the

99 LED CLONES

'80s overlooked. And that would be the *sound* of Zeppelin, and in particular, John Bonham's instantly-recognizable drum sound. For much of Zep's studio recordings, it seemed like it was all about getting an authentic live sound...while their disciples (and the album producers) completely bypassed this important element.

To get a sense of what I'm getting at here, do a Pepsi taste test between say, Zeppelin's "In My Time of Dying" and then Bonham's "Wait for You," Zeppelin's "Black Dog" followed by Whitesnake's "Still of the Night," and then wrap it all up with a good old fashioned dose of Zeppelin's "Good Time Bad Times" and chase it down with Kingdom Come's "Get It On." Again, I'm not talking about how similar some of the musical parts sound. I'm just speaking strictly from a *sonic* perspective, where Zep sounds like it was recorded all in one take at a grotty rehearsal space, while the other bands' music sounds as if it was pristinely recorded track upon track upon track in a high-priced, spotless studio – with interns racing around to fetch the next requested cappuccino.

Eddie Trunk seems to agree with this sonic observation...and further explored how/why it happened. "As time goes on, it just becomes things with technology. I think people figure stuff out from a technology standpoint – 'Hey, let's try doing this. Maybe we can get that sound not by mic'ing the drums a certain way, but now there's these samples and drum triggers.' And now you've got digital recording and all these different things that come into play. So, I think for a lot of musicians, the palette to paint on got bigger and wider. And all of this technology came into play that Zeppelin never had. I mean, Zeppelin was done in terms of recording by 1980. The '80s were a *huge* change where digital came in and sampling and all these other things. So, I think that played a big role in people moving away from it, or trying to maybe build off of that – but then expand on that and make it their own."

Badland's Greg Chaisson also seems to agree that many of the Led Clones failed to replicate the drum thunder of Bonzo. "When you listen to Kingdom Come – and they weren't trying to be a Zeppelin influence, *they were trying to channel Zeppelin the whole way* – I thought the drum sound was a little disappointing. A band that had some Zeppelin in them that I thought did a pretty good job with the sounds of the record were a couple of those early Black Crowes records, which have a little Zeppelin bent to them, and they kept the drums sounding more real."

Also, Chaisson explained why Eric Singer's drum style on Badlands' self-titled debut stood out from the rest of the pack circa the late '80s. "Eric's approach from a drumming perspective had an obvious 'Bonham bent,' but the thing is he did it so well. At the time in LA, there were three kinds of drummers – a Tommy Lee clone, a Tommy Aldridge clone, and a John Bonham clone. And I don't think Eric is a clone of any of those, because Eric's influences are so diverse. I definitely think that in the songs that are required to have that kind of feel, Eric did it very well."

And it turns out that John Paul Jones could also tell the difference between two eras, shortly after the dawn of the '90s, and even pinpointed the main reason – when he once explained in an MTV interview, "Bonzo's favorite music was actually the slower Motown stuff. It was either James Brown or the real sweet soul music that he loved. This is why all those bands that supposedly sound like us never get it right, because it's all 'Mmm…BASH…mmm…BASH!' If you listen to what Bonzo did, he had all this little stuff in it."

Even the manager/songwriter of Great White, Alan Niven, mirrored Jones' sentiment. "What Zeppelin had that Great White didn't have is John Bonham. And drummers drive guitar players. That's one thing that you cannot

101 LED CLONES

replicate – because Bonham had a power and a feel that is very rarely well-matched. There are drummers that have heavy hands, but Bonham could hit hard and still swing. And Bonham had dynamics of when he really drove something, it was unstoppable."

With all this sudden Bonzo chit-chat, now is as good a time as ever to bring up an obvious question…how did Bonham get such an outstanding drum sound in the studio with Zeppelin? Quite a few drum experts explained this in my 2020 book, *BONZO: 30 Rock Drummers Remember the Legendary John Bonham.* And first up, is a quote from Anthrax's Charlie Benante.

"I think it was all in his wrists. I also know for a fact – because just in reading everything I possibly could on Led Zeppelin through the years – how he would put headphones on when they were recording, and didn't use many mics on his kit. But the mics that he did use were placed in a certain way that when he heard it back, it sounded exactly how he heard it when he sat there. So, sometimes when you hear drums mixed on a record, they may sound like a little disproportionate type of thing, because the toms don't sound as equal as the snare or kick. But with him, everything was mixed really well and compressed, so the triplets always came out sounding correct. And he was totally on top of that."

Benante also discussed one of Bonham's best-known drum bits – and how he obtained its classic sound. "I heard two different stories about how they got the 'When the Levee Breaks' sound. There's one story that said his drum kit was delivered at the house that they were recording – Headley Grange – and he was so excited that he put them right in the hall where they were delivered to, and set them up right there. Jimmy heard that, and said, 'Don't touch them!' And I guess they mic'd it from a staircase up, and put a few more mics down there too, and that's how they got that sound. That's one version of it, which sounds like it could have been that way."

"The second version was I heard that they spent time on it, micing and different techniques – putting it out of phase, putting it in phase. I heard all the other stories about it. But I heard it was that Ludwig kit that got delivered – and I guess that was the green sparkle kit."

And according to one of Bonzo's former drum techs, Jeff Ocheltree, many who attempt to duplicate his instantly recognizable style and sound often falter, because they don't understand his drumming background. "He listened to a lot of swing – he was a swinger. I mean, that guy could swing. And he listened to jazz drummers of the old days and how they maybe had no mics or one mic, and he understood the dynamics of big drums and how to get them to project. First of all – he was a great player. Self-taught. And, he listened to a lot of jazz-fusion, Latin music."

Additionally, Ocheltree explained it was what Bonham *didn't* play that also became part of his style. "Expression – I think John Bonham was a genius when it came to expressing himself on certain tunes. There were gaps in the way that he would lay it out, sometimes. And just enough gap to make it dynamic. And not a lot of guys were doing that. Everybody talks about 'Good Times Bad Times' – the bass drum playing. But when you listen to all those records of Zeppelin, he really had a unique, uncanny ability of knowing when to lay back a little bit and when to put himself in there. Just a very unique situation, because like I said, he was self-taught. I don't know that he ever had a lesson."

Also in that aforementioned *BONZO* book, I asked a few interviewees about why so many of the '80s era Led Clones committed the same repeated flub in the drum

103 LED CLONES

department – going for an '80s sound rather than a '70s one – and ex-Scorpions drummer Herman Rarebell, shared his thoughts on the topic. "I think that when you are a drummer and you wanted to copy Bonham, then you find out how difficult it was really to play those riffs – what he did. Especially if you have songs like 'Good Times Bad Times' – where he was the first one to do with one foot pedal what normal drummers do with two bass drums."

Rarebell even added his thoughts about the struggle Bonham's own son must have experienced later on. "But nobody has come close so far to copying Bonham – even his son, Jason, who I met first at the Moscow Music Peace Festival [in 1989], when he was in his early twenties. Even he was asked from Led Zeppelin to do concerts, and you could hear that his father is his father. But he was not his father...he was the son. It is a similar situation with Julian Lennon and John Lennon. All those kids have to live in the shadow of their fathers. Unfortunately, they are not like their father. There is just one Bonham, I think. He was a unique drummer that gets born every hundred years, so to speak."

Charlie Benante also pointed out that most "Led children" of the '80s "Tried to do it more vocally and musically" – rather than trying to replicate Bonham's massive drum sound. Which again, after such drum bashers as Bobby Chouinard and Eric Carr *did* manage to reproduce that trademark booming sound in the early '80s, it seemed like most drummers afterwards were simply not up for the challenge – and became slaves to technology.

Also, Rik Emmett observed how many of these aforementioned Zep mimics failed to observe and learn from the many different musical facets of the band – and also, the brilliance of their rhythm section. "The things about Zeppelin that I loved was when reggae would find its way into what they were doing musically [the song 'D'yer

Mak'er']. That there would be funk that would find its way into what they were doing [the songs 'The Crunge' and 'Trampled Underfoot']. So, if there's a 'Zeppelin band' and they don't have those things, then I kind of go, 'Well...I think you're missing the boat here'."

"There were things that Bonham did that he could swing the way Jeff Porcaro from Toto could swing and the way Bernard Purdie could ['Fool in the Rain']. There were things that Zeppelin did because of the musicianship in the band that Steely Dan did. So, if a band is just copying two or three of the dimensions of Led Zeppelin but not the multi-dimensions of it, then I kind of go, 'You're not picking up musically on what this band was. They were capable of *a lot* of stuff'."

"I would say to many musicians, 'Don't listen to Zeppelin and just listen to Jimmy and Robert. You've got to listen to what that rhythm section was capable of.' That bass player is *phenomenal*. And some of the things that he plays, like the bass part in 'Ramble On,' it's genius. And the little voicings he plays on the Mellotron in 'Stairway to Heaven' that's the recorders at the beginning – he was like a genius when he played that part. The voicings and the way he made it grow...*it was genius*."

Oh, and by the way, we mustn't forget a couple of other "Bonzo-like bashers" that we have yet to truly touch upon. First up, Cozy Powell, who was best known for his work with Jeff Beck, Rainbow, and Black Sabbath. As Kenny Aronoff once stated, "Cozy Powell was a John Bonham duplicate. Unbelievable how he emulated Bonham. His sound, his feel – he got it real good."

"I think Cozy was from the same school as the John Bonhams," Charlie Benante also once theorized. "But I think that Cozy did it with...a little more testosterone. He had two kick drums instead of one, and he brought this severe low-

105 LED CLONES

end to the mix. His playing was so heavy. He played so right for the songs, too. *Like John Bonham.* But Cozy, the beginning of [Rainbow's] 'Stargazer,' to me, was always one of my favorite intros - a great drum intro. To this day. I was just listening to it a couple of days ago, and it still makes the hair on my arms stand up."

And if you remember, Eddie Trunk mentioned Y&T's Leonard Haze earlier, and was willing to explore the subject a bit more in-depth. "You mentioned Bobby Chouinard. Leonard Haze – very similar to that, in a guy very much known for a huge pocket and his mastery of the kick drum and using his right foot…or left foot, depending on the drummer. Guys that didn't necessarily have a massive kit and played a single kick drum, and just laid down that groove. Played a little bit behind the beat. And Leonard Haze absolutely was *worshipped* by drummers. Y&T went through some line-up changes, and no matter who they ended up getting on drums, it was always like, 'Well…there's only one Leonard'. He's definitely a Bonham descendent in my opinion."

So, that about does it for this extensive discussion of the '80s. *Phew.* I don't think I ever analyzed (over-analyzed?) Zeppelin and their influence on others as much as I did in these past few chapters. Hopefully, we all learned a thing or two from it. Me? I'm going to take a breather for a bit and fold my laundry. But I promise to return shortly…

CHAPTER VIII
THE '90s

OK, so, the '90s began with two semi-Zep reunions. The first one was a private affair – which occurred on April 28, 1990 at Jason Bonham's wedding at the Heath Hotel in Bewdley, England, which was attended by all three surviving Zeplanders (plus a surprisingly svelte-looking Peter Grant). And at one point during the wedding party, Page, Plant, and Jones joined the younger Bonham for a jam of the tunes "Custard Pie," "It'll Be Me," "Rock and Roll," "Sick Again," and "Bring It On Home."

And the second was an enormously public affair – Jimmy Page joining Robert Plant for three Zep tunes during Plant's solo performance as part of the multi-artist Silver Clef Winners concert at Knebworth (which also featured Paul McCartney, Pink Floyd, and Genesis, among others), on June 30, 1990. The songs performed between the two (with Plant's backing band providing the necessary backing)? "Misty Mountain Hop," the first-ever live rendition of "Wearing and Tearing," and a set-closing "Rock and Roll." The consensus? *By far* the best Zep one-off reunion to ever occur up to this point, due in large point to the strength, energy, and tightness of the noble men backing Page and Plant. Who, I'm quite certain were guitarist Doug Boyle, bassist Charlie Jones, keyboardist Phil Johnstone, and drummer Chris Blackwell. Kudos, gentlemen!

However, similarly to Live Aid and the Atlantic Records performances, these two 1990 mini-sets led to no Led reunion. As a result, Atlantic Records did the next best thing to generate some more income from their golden goose…a box set. Up to this point, there was never a compilation of Zep's best bits – making them the ultimate "album band" (in other words, if you wanted to obtain

107 LED CLONES

"Stairway to Heaven," you'd better save your allowance to purchase *Led Zeppelin IV,* as there was no 45 single nor compilation to take a short-cut to).

But instead of issuing a single-disc "best of" – which would have proven to be the most lucrative – a decision was made to embrace the suddenly-thriving "box set" format. And with the popularity of the compact disc quickly usurping vinyl and cassette popularity-wise, what better time than now to scour through the Zep discography and boil it all down to four CD's full of favorites (and six LP's and four cassettes for those holding on to apparent fast-fading formats). Simply titled *Led Zeppelin* and issued on October 8, 1990 – wisely just in time for the holiday season – the box helped ignite another wave of "Zep mania," as a pair of videos were aired heavily on MTV ("Travelling Riverside Blues" and "Over the Hills and Far Away"). As expected, the set sold like hotcakes worldwide – eventually earning an esteemed diamond certification in the US (2,500,000 copies sold x 4 CD's = 10,000,000 total sold).

Also, there was one last gasp for '80s-styled Zep disciples – Slaughter's bombastic/syrupy power ballad, "Fly to the Angels." Issued as a single in 1990 (from their double platinum-certified debut LP, *Stick It to Ya*), the tune featured Mark Slaughter's unmistakably Plant-esque vocals and a Zep-like symphonic bit in the middle thrown in for good measure. At the very least, "Angels" served as a "door closer" for "Get It On"/"Still of the Night"-styled Zep pupils. So, at least the tune had that going for it. Additionally in 1990, one of the world's leading metal bands, Iron Maiden, covered Zep's "Communication Breakdown" as the b-side of their "Bring Your Daughter…to the Slaughter" single.

But it was also around the dawn of the '90s that Plant explained what he disliked about heavy metal bands of that era. "It's lack of consideration for the consumer. In other words, there's so much fake shit around. You know very well and I know very well that so many people take it as a career move and as a career alone to please people by doing the most obvious thing."

But he did name-check a few up-and-coming metal acts at the time that stood out from the rest of the pack. "People like Faith No More and Prong and Jane's Addiction and Soundgarden – they are to me what is important about aggressive music. But the hollow gestures of so many…" And it turns out that Plant *really* fancied Faith No More. "I think their first album is absolutely stunning. I think their first album caught, they just rode two styles and those two styles fucked each other to such a degree it worked perfectly. More than that, it was a shock. It was great to hear. *Introduce Yourself* was one of the greatest pieces of music I'd heard in years."

With so many bloody artists of the past few years plagiarizing Zep, it was only a matter of time until someone injected some humor into their approach. And that time came with the arrival of Dread Zeppelin in 1990, and their debut full-length, *Un-Led-Ed*. As DZ's name suggests, the band specialized in covers of Zep tunes that were reconstructed as reggae-rock numbers. But the best part of it all was that the band was fronted by a bloody Elvis impersonator, who went by the name of Tortelvis (real name: Greg Tortell) – who sang the tunes in a King-like manner!

And the group's best number happened to go by the name of "Heartbreaker (At the End of Lonely Street)," which combined the lyrics of Presley's "Heartbreak Hotel" with the music of Zep's "Heartbreaker" – for which a music video was shot, to boot. Which brings to mind…shouldn't Weird Al Yankovic have tackled a Zep-like spoof around this time? A missed opportunity, if you ask me.

However, by 1991, it was becoming clearer by the

109 LED CLONES

day that there was a change on the horizon within rock music – with the emergence of alternative rock and grunge. The difference? Both styles were a reaction against the largely-unbearable hair metal bands of the '80s – with most alt-rockers/grungers dressing down, the importance of quality songwriting (and the message of your lyrics), choosing second-hand guitars over shredding away on your over-priced pointy instrument, etc. And it just so happened that many groups from the alt-rockin' early '90s were major fans of Zep. But, unlike many of the '80s Zep admirers, only used their admiration as a starting point – before ultimately putting their own unique spin on things.

But the most obvious difference was how grunge/alt artists wisely rejected the awful canon drums and glossy sounds of the '80s Zepster bands, and embraced a rawer and live sonic approach in their recordings – much more like the sound of a band setting up microphones in their rehearsal studio and letting it rip. As a result, the sonics were much more a kin to *Physical Graffiti* than, oh say, *The Disregard of Timekeeping*.

The first band that we'll discuss that received a comparison to Zeppelin (vocally) and Sabbath (musically) was Soundgarden. But it seems as though the "familiarity" only occurred early in the Seattle/grunge band's recording career – namely, a specific song on their 1988 offering, *Ultramega OK*. "They came out with a song, 'Incessant Mace,' which was flat-out stolen from 'Dazed and Confused' by Led Zeppelin," a chap who was part of the scene at the time, Leighton Beezer, once told me for the book *Grunge Is Dead: The Oral History of Seattle Rock Music*. "Not even a little bit. But it was twelve minutes long, heavier than shit – Led Zeppelin didn't play small clubs. [Laughs] It was like, "God, this is a rip, but…y'know, they're really good!"

Also in the same book, another bloke that was part of

the local scene at the time, Rod Moody, recalled, "I saw one of Soundgarden's early shows at a place called Scoundrel's Lair. Chris Cornell later claimed that Led Zeppelin had no effect on him, but they played at least *three* Zep songs back to back." But there were also others who felt that any similarity between the two was merely by coincidence, including their former soundman, Stu Hallerman. "Kim [Thayil] did not like bands like Led Zeppelin, and Hiro [Yamamoto] didn't like rock n' roll at all as a teenager. So everyone at the time was like, 'Oh, obviously these guys are a Led Zeppelin rip-off,' when whatever resemblance they had was really natural – that's just the way they hit their guitars and screamed. It was a coincidence more than anything. I think we all came to like Led Zeppelin at some point in our lives, but it was not a direct influence for them."

However, Thayil himself once recounted to me that Soundgarden's supposed resemblance to Zeppelin once proved harmful to the band – when they were opening a show early on for Faith No More. "We did the gig opening for them in an area of Vancouver called Gastown, at a small bar. A couple of things I remember about that was sometime during the middle of the set, Chris said he heard someone say, *'Fucking Led Zeppelin crap,'* and then threw a glass ashtray that shattered on Matt Cameron's kick drum. I remember hearing the thud and the crack. Which is kind of fucked up, and whoever did that, could have seriously gotten their fucking ass kicked by the band. But we weren't really the kind of band that would cower, so what we did was we just moved to the front of the stage and played even louder and more aggressively. That kind of shit got us more aggressive and combative. And almost always, we won them over."

Additionally, in 2011, Chris Cornell performed an

outstanding bare bones version of Zep's "Thank You" (consisting of just vocals and acoustic guitar) that was included on his *Thank You* live solo album. He would also perform the tune on *The Howard Stern Show* that same year, and explained why he chose that tune from all the other gems of the Zep song catalog. "It was kind of almost uncharacteristic of other stuff off that album. It sounds like a '60s pop song to me – the way that they have it arranged. And it's almost like that would have been – with any other band – their biggest hit. But because it was Led Zeppelin and the album was so unbelievable, it's their first album [actually, *Led Zeppelin II*, but please continue...] you almost kind of pass over it."

And upon listening to Cornell's version of "Thank You," it suddenly becomes crystal clear that this is the perfect example of a rock artist covering a Zeppelin tune and not merely copying the song's original composers – most obvious being that Cornell sings in his own voice, not the "Plant approximation" that such vocalists as say, Lenny Wolf or Daniel MacMaster favored in the late '80s.

And what did a member of one of the late '80s Zep-esque bands think of Soundgarden? Badlands' Greg Chaisson was willing to share his thoughts. "Chris Cornell obviously was a great singer and a lot of those bands had interesting things. But when I listen to that, if there's any Zeppelin influence in that, it's more of the primitive Zeppelin influence. When you listen to Soundgarden, he sonically had more to do with the dirgy Sabbath kind of thing. I know Ray [Gillen] was a big fan of it. He'd bring in Soundgarden and go, 'This guy can *really* sing.' So, he was a huge Chris Cornell fan."

And although you don't necessarily think "Led Zeppelin" when you hear the top grunge band of all-time, Nirvana, it turns out that they were clearly admirers – most obvious by Dave Grohl's John Bonham "3 circle symbol" being tattooed on his arm, and also, the title of their early obscurity, "Aero Zeppelin," which was included on their 1992 odds n' ends comp, *Incesticide*. When I once asked early Nirvana drummer Chad Channing about the track, he was willing to help fill in some of the blanks concerning this mysterious tune. "It was Dale [Crover] – he did the first demos that had 'Aero Zeppelin.' Kurt [Cobain] actually gave me the demo when I joined the band. I think it was great. The title, I remember thinking, 'That's a unique name for a song,' and then I listened to it, and was like, 'That's pretty cool.' You can definitely see where Kurt had fun with the idea, matching ideas together, I suppose."

Another Zep tie-in with Nirvana was that their two best-known drummers Channing (who played on 1989's *Bleach*) and Grohl (who played on 1991's *Nevermind* and 1993's *In Utero*) both greatly admired Bonzo's big drum sound. "We were always looking to get that big drum sound," Channing admitted. "And of course, John Bonham most of the time played that big 26-inch kick drum – just this huge kick drum. And the production, they got great recorded sounds for the drums."

Along with the box set, another incredibly popular format during the '90s – and an easy way for record companies to make a quick buck – was the "tribute album," in which various renowned artists covered tunes from one of rock's greats, neatly compiled onto a single release. And by 1995, it was the Led men's turn in line, with the release of *Encomium: A Tribute to Led Zeppelin*. And featured on it were two standout alt-rock artists of the era that managed to enjoy Zeppelin, without getting weighed down with too much Led – Blind Melon and Stone Temple Pilots.

In the case of Blind Melon, the band – who was largely considered "alt-rock" due to some Jane's Addiction-

113 LED CLONES

like moments, but probably had more in common stylistically with the southern rock of the '70s – did indeed show off a Zep moment or two even before the arrival of *Encomium*, such as the guitar riff featured in "Seed to a Tree" off their 1992 self-titled debut. Also, unlike some Zep-like bands that drew the wrath of Robert Plant in the previous decade, the one-time Golden God liked what he heard – and saw – from Blind Melon, as he once was quoted as saying, "I've never seen them before, but they're just amazing. They take the music off into uncharted places. They really have what it takes. Are they playing anywhere else while they're over here? I think they're so good I have to catch them again."

But when the time arrived for Blind Melon to select a tune to cover for *Encomium*, they opted to take on one of the more obscure rockers Zep ever offered – "Out on the Tiles" off *Led Zeppelin III*. Recorded in Bearsville Studios with former Zep engineer Eddie Kramer overseeing the sessions, Melon guitarist Rogers Stevens recalled, "We had always talked about how we were into Led Zeppelin, and then found out that Robert Plant liked the band. He came to a show or two in England. I was kind of disappointed in the way it came out, but it was cool. It was a hard song to do – there's a lot of tough, deceptively difficult rhythmic things in that song. We kind of glossed over them and didn't do them."

"I think it was a high song [to sing]. I remember [Shannon Hoon] having a hard time getting the vocal, and that was before the days of Auto-Tune – when you could go in, fake it, and then fix it. He actually had to sing it and it was a struggle – but we got it. I remember Eddie Kramer pulling out all these photographs – the guy worked on the Hendrix records, he engineered the original Zeppelin recording of that song. He has loads of photographs – intimate studio pictures of everyone from Zeppelin to

Hendrix. Killer stuff that you've never seen before." Sadly, after only one more album, 1995's oft-overlooked gem, *Soup*, Blind Melon would split in the wake of singer Shannon Hoon's death shortly after the album's release (before reuniting with singer Travis Warren in 2006).

Another alt-rock outfit thriving around the same time was Stone Temple Pilots. And while singer Scott Weiland didn't sing like Plant (he was actually criticized at the time for sounding too darn much like Pearl Jam's Eddie Vedder), guitarist Dean DeLeo was certainly well-versed in Zep guitar riffs and grooves, case in point, "Plush," as well as the lesser known "Sin" – both off their hit 1992 debut, *Core*. And while the latter tune features monolithic riffing, there is also a breakdown part in the middle which includes some Zoso-like acoustic strumming (and again, unlike the pristine production of the '80s era, featured a much more organic/live sound – which worked wonders). Which interestingly, reflected a quote Page once offered – concerning composing memorable riffs. "In the Zeppelin era, a lot of the music was riff-led. But there was this other, more acoustic element. 'Ten Years Gone' was totally different, with an orchestrated-guitar element."

When I once asked STP drummer Eric Kretz if the producer of their hit albums from the '90s, Brendan O'Brien, modeled his productions after Zep, he admitted so right off the bat. "Definitely. Because Brendan is the same age as us. So, he grew up with the same thing on all the great, classic – mostly British – bands from the '70s. But he definitely had a fondness for how those records were made. And it's kind of within his amazing use of the midrange. Brendan's records have such a good focus on the midrange – which is how Zeppelin made records, as well."

"Especially by the time we got to *Purple* – our second album – Brendan was like, 'Oh...that would be *this*

115 LED CLONES

kind of amp.' He'd pull out all little amps, and would say, 'Jimmy would use this on *this kind* of song, and Jimmy would use this on *that kind* of song.' Because the first record, we were just so excited to be making a record that we kind of had somewhat of a grasp on our equipment, but by the time we made our second record, everybody was buying gear left and right. So, we couldn't wait to try out new tones. And of course, all those tones basically harken back to what Zeppelin were putting together."

And come *Encomium* time, the opener of the second side of *Houses of the Holy,* was chosen/covered by the Pilots. But instead of simply replicating the tune, they deconstructed it in a laid-back, folky manner – with an outstanding vocal performance from Weiland. And similar to the aforementioned Chris Cornell version of "Thank You," Weiland opts to not go all "Plant-y" vocally – which again shows how '90s alt-rockers influenced by Zep didn't take the easy way out…unlike many the decade before. The end result? Quite possibly yours truly's favorite Zep cover of all-time (perhaps only second behind King Curtis & the Kingpins' rendition of "Whole Lotta Love" from way back in 1970).

"Whenever you try to approach doing a cover of a classic song – something like 'Dancing Days' – it's kind of like sacred ground," Kretz once admitted. "So, you're apprehensive about doing it, but then we could justify it by doing it in a different form – doing a more acoustic thing with it. And Scott's more of a tenor range on it. We approached it totally different and it was really fun to record it that way. You kind of know how the song sounds in your head, but recording a lot of new music in the studio, you know how you want the song to sound, but until it's finally mixed, you're not 100% aware of where the song is traveling to."

"But growing up and having songs like 'Dancing Days' so ingrained in your brain...you kind of knew the feel and energy of it – you already knew it was going to be a great song to start with. What we wanted to do was not compete with it and try to do it in the same manner – because why would you even attempt that, unless it was just for fun?" Sadly, similar to Hoon, Weiland was not long for this world, passing away in 2015 (with STP carrying on with other vocalists – first Linkin Park's Chester Bennington, and then Jeff Gutt).

Also in the early '90s, an emergence of "retro rock" artists began to flourish – probably tops of all being Leonard Albert Kravitz. And as he had an unmistakable fondness for '70s rock artists (both musically and fashion-wise), of course, some Zep Led into his tunes – such as his 1991 collaboration with Guns N' Roses' Slash, "Always on the Run" (off the album *Mama Said*).

And Kravitz once explained how the union took place. "I went to high school with Slash and then I saw him at the *American Music Awards*. I invited him in the studio to do the solo on 'Fields of Joy,' and then we decided to write a song together. He was on tour in Europe. After the last date, he jumped on the Concorde and flew from London to New York at nine in the morning. He had me get a gallon of vodka and a bag of ice, and we went in the studio and bang, there it was. The two of us wrote and cut the tune."

"I played drums; he played guitar; then I played my guitar, bass and did the vocals. I brought the horn players in and it was done. Then he got on a plane the next morning and went to LA. It was a wild day. The lyrics are about how my mom always wanted to give me her wisdom. She would want me to slow down sometimes to think and take things in. I was just on a crazy ride at the time and couldn't slow down. She was telling me this stuff at the time…'but I'm

117 LED CLONES

always on the run'."

But probably Kravitz's best known/best tasting "Zeppole" was the title track from his 1993 LP, *Are You Gonna Go My Way* – particularly the guitar riff. "That song was literally cut in five minutes," Kravitz once recalled. "My session was getting ready to end and another band was coming in. The song was something that came really quick. Craig Ross and I went in there and cut it, bang. I played the drums, he was on the guitar and my bass player at the time, Tony Breit, was on it. We cut it live. We didn't have time to take it in. I took the cassette home and listened and listened and listened and was like, 'What am I gonna do with this?' Then the melody and the words came. I went back to the studio the next day and sang it. I had no idea what I had." And if you closely paid attention to Kravitz's performance of the tune at the 1993 MTV Video Music Awards, you would have spotted a familiar face on bass…John Paul Jones!

And a tune off his next album, 1995's *Circus*, entitled "Rock and Roll Is Dead," also contained a very Led-y guitar riff. In fact, when Kravitz graced the cover of the November 30, 1995 issue of *Rolling Stone,* writer Neil Strauss grilled him with a flurry of questions – including flat out accusing him of ripping off the *Zep II* ditty "Living Loving Maid (She's Just a Woman)" for his tune. And the final part of the conversation ended with Strauss interrogating, "So you don't think the introduction to that song sounds anything like 'Living Loving Maid'?" To which Kravitz responded, "No, I mean, I think it has a Zeppelin-type quality. Oh, I don't know. Let's not talk about it."

Years later, Kravitz would also admit to receiving some valuable career advice from a former member of Zeppelin circa 1993, when Robert Plant opted to open shows for Kravitz. "I was doing a soundcheck, and I guess I was in a bit of a mood because I didn't like the way the stage sounded that night, and Robert ripped into me and tore me apart, basically saying: 'What the fuck is wrong with you? You're in the middle of this great success, you have this music, you're having a great run and you should be enjoying every moment. Let go, relax!' He was yelling at me like he was my older brother or my dad or something!"

"It freaked me out and I was a little embarrassed. Here was one of my heroes telling me what a bitch I'm being. But it was the most beautiful thing, because he's a real guy and he saw me in this wonderful place that he's been, and he said: 'You better fucking wake up and enjoy this and have fun.' And that turned me around. We've been great friends ever since." Kravitz would eventually get an opportunity to thank Plant for his helpful advice way back when – when he paid tribute to Zeppelin by singing "Whole Lotta Love" at the aforementioned Kennedy Center Honors on December 2, 2012 (with Plant, Page, and Jones all in attendance).

Also during the '90s, several artists hit the charts with a style that merged hard rock with funk – including the aforementioned Mr. Kravitz, but probably best-known of all, the Red Hot Chili Peppers. And while they started out as a self-described "punk funk" band, by the time they arrived at their commercial breakthrough album, 1991's *Blood Sugar Sex Magik*, they had suddenly began inserting Zep-worthy guitar riffs into some of their tunes courtesy of John Frusciante, most obviously the tune "Suck My Kiss" (and while it may not be Zep-like, the riff included in the album's title track is simply one of best/most underrated of all-time). And who was the producer of *BSSM*? None other than the same man who inserted Zep samples into Beastie Boys tunes and encouraged the Cult to embrace their inner Zep way back when – Rick Rubin.

Another '90s band that walked the line between rock and funk was Primus – led by singer/bassist Les Claypool.

119 LED CLONES

And while Primus' best known albums, such as 1991's *Sailing the Seas of Cheese*, didn't particularly trample any Zep-isms underfoot, that all changed later in the decade – not compositionally, but *sonically*. And in particular, with their underrated 1997 offering, *Brown Album*. And Claypool admitted as much when I interviewed him for the 2014 book, *Primus, Over the Electric Grapevine: Insight into Primus and the World of Les Claypool*.

"The *Brown Album* was definitely the-monkeys-running-the-asylum time – times a hundred. We took our advance and we bought a bunch of equipment and a recording console. We wanted to get it back into analog, so we went and bought this one-inch sixteen-track machine, and this console. Basically, we went in and tried to make like a *Physical Graffiti*-sounding record. And we're in there overloading microphones and clipping compressors, and all kinds of shit."

"It's funny, because I remember Tom Waits telling me that the *Brown Album* was his favorite Primus record because it sounds like it needs a good wash. I've listened to it again fairly recently, and it *is* the *Brown Album* – it's this dark, kind of dirty creature that sort of wafts through your speakers. One of the things Brain asked when he came in the band was, 'Hey, do I need to play all this double bass stuff?' And we were like, 'No! We're going in a new direction here. You don't have to do any of that.' So he bought these giant drums – not multiple drums, but huge in size. Kind of like Bonham. This old jelly bean kit. And we recorded this thing, and it was a conscious decision to go in the polar opposite direction than we had gone before with the percussion."

As Claypool mentioned, the *Brown Album* was Primus' first without then-recently departed drummer Tim "Herb" Alexander, who was replaced by Bryan "Brain" Mantia, the latter of which also shared his memories of recording sessions and their new Zep direction. "Les's whole concept was, 'Tim used this huge drum set, with all these high drums and crazy cymbals. Why don't we just go totally opposite? Just use a Bonham-sounding kit. And let's go directly to tape, let's don't use any digital stuff. Let's go real balls-out, heavy, big-groove, kind of distressed sound, and make this album'."

"And he said, 'Let's call it the *Brown Album*. And we were like, 'Sounds good. Let's do it!' That's how we approached it – we just approached it totally the opposite of everything they did before. Everything was big drums. We were looking at pictures of John Bonham's kit and mic'ing it the same way. And Les had this way of recording a drum where he put a mic right behind your head where your ear is, and he'd put a sock over it, and it just had this muffled, compressed sound."

Other alt-rockers of the '90s era who "got it right" in sprinkling a pinch – rather than a punch – of Zeppelin into their approach would also include Jane's Addiction ("Pigs in Zen"), Living Colour ("Desperate People"), Masters of Reality ("V.H.V."), Mother Love Bone ("Heartshine"), Rage Against the Machine ("Vietnow"), and Jeff Buckley (his deconstructed cover of Zep's "Night Flight"), among others. Also bands of the genre that although most of their tunes did not reflect Zep, did offer up a tune or two that did (the music contained in the Stone Roses' "Love Spreads" could certainly be filed in this category).

And with rock artists getting back to a much more live sound production-wise, did the former members of Zep follow suit with their own recordings in the early to mid-part of the '90s? Yes and no. Concerning Robert Plant, two solo efforts arrived during this time, 1990's *Manic Nirvana* (which merrily continued on in the same direction as his previous solo offerings) and 1993's *Fate of the Nations* (which scaled back the unmistakably '80s production somewhat, evidenced most in the removal of "big canon drums"). John Paul Jones on the other band seemed to be fully aware of what was going on around him musically and adjusted accordingly – by working with such challenging/original artists as the Butthole Surfers (producing their 1993 LP, *Independent Worm Saloon*) and Diamanda Galás (collaborating, playing, and producing 1994's *The Sporting Life*), as well as arranging orchestration for REM (1992's *Automatic for the People*).

Jimmy Page? Well, the famous phrase "if you can't beat 'em, join 'em" certainly came into play – when he was paired with none other than David Coverdale, for a short-lived venture that simply went by the name of "Coverdale Page." The story goes that supposedly Mr. Page sought a Zeppelin reunion in the wake of the success of the group's box set, but was rebuffed by Mr. Plant. Instead of sitting around on his toches and doing diddly, Page apparently sought the aid of Geffen A&R executive John Kalodner (who played a major role in the "rebirth" of Aerosmith in the late '80s), who suggested he collaborate with Coverdale, who at that point had put Whitesnake into hibernation.

"In essence, Jimmy was dying to get back into it," Coverdale recalled. "At the same time, I was dying to get out of it. I'd had enough of all the peripheral stuff, stuff which in the music business seems to be as important as the songs; the videos, the press, the photo sessions, the looking-like-a-girly-man stuff. I'd really had enough, so privately, without telling anybody, I'd actually retired at the end of 1990. I'd really lost perspective on whether I personally had the passion to keep going, for a multitude of reasons; a great deal to do with personal circumstances."

And Page gave his side of the story around the same time. "After the *Outrider* album, I wanted to do a really big album, and get out on the road and show I was still alive and kicking, basically. I'd been wading through scores of cassettes of singers, and it was getting pretty daunting. I wasn't getting any inspiration at all, and then I got a call saying, 'Would you consider working with David?'."

After a meeting between the duo in NYC during March 1991, a decision was made – the collaboration was indeed a good idea. "We just went behind locked doors and started writing, and kept everything very private," recalled Page. "All the speculation went on outside those locked doors, and it certainly wasn't fueled by us. There was bound to be speculation as soon as it was even leaked that the two of us were working together. People had preconceived notions of what it was going to be…" Coverdale on the other hand, offered perhaps the most fitting – and admirably honest – description of the material that they cooked up, by simply stating, "Led Snake," in a chat with *Kerrang!* at the time.

Recorded from 1991-1992 in several different studios and with production being handled by Coverdale, Page, and a chap by the name of Mike Fraser, the duo's debut offering was a self-titled one issued on March 15, 1993. Now, I have a confession to make, which may knock your socks off – until working on this very book, I had never listened to the *Coverdale Page* album in its entirety. Why? Because at that point in my life, I was knee-deep in the now-classic '90s alt-rock recordings that were rearing their heads at that precise point. And also as I confessed earlier, I was suffering from a severe case of "Zep burnout" (add to it the fact that I was never a big "Whitesnake guy," although I do quite fancy Coverdale's three LP's with Deep Purple), and was taking a bit of a break from the band that seemed to have a thing for dogs – both black and/or hot.

Listening to the album with a set of "2024 ears,"

123 LED CLONES

here are my thoughts and concerns about what I heard, track by track:

- "Shake My Tree": Plant-y vocals, although includes some impressive acoustic guitar doodling by Page...before the "big riffing" begins.

- "Waiting on You": *Eh*.

- "Take Me for a Little While": A ballad that sounds at the beginning like it could have been included on *Slide It In*, before it leads directly into '80s power ballad territory, complete with those dreaded "canon drums." Which leads one to wonder...if Bonham didn't pass when he did and continued merrily along throughout the '80s, would he have also fallen victim to the "canon craze," or would he have had the wherewithal to stand firm and retain his trademark booming/organic/live sound? I'd like to think he would have turned a deaf ear to it, but with everyone and their mother at the time thinking it was a good idea...who knows?

- "Pride and Joy": The only tune I remember hearing (and seeing, thanks to its music video) at the time, and it sounds precisely like Coverdale's earlier "Led Snake" comment/description.

- "Over Now": My selection as best tune of the entire album, as it is an example of the collaboration getting it right, due to interesting/dark music – not riff-based – and Coverdale singing in his own pre-1987 style. Also, good use of strings – not in an expected "Kashmir" manner, but adding to the foreboding feel of the music.

- "Feeling Hot": Sounds like a Whitesnake reject, which contains a cliched/Spinal Tap-worthy lyric: "Women to the left, women to the right." The music is the same sorta rock boogie woogie a la Van Halen's "Hot for Teacher," and even includes a stacked vocalization that is unmistakably Def Leppard-like, which comes out of nowhere mid-way through.

- "Easy Does It": Breaks one of the cardinal rules (or rather, *commits the cardinal sin*) of rock lyric writing, where Mr. Coverdale dares to use the phrase "promised land" – which he then rhymes with the word "understand." Kids, please – learn from this mistake and never commit this flagrant flub.

- "Take a Look at Yourself": Please consult my above description of "Waiting on You."

- "Don't Leave Me This Way": Coverdale pulls a total "Plant" and apes his trademark "Baby, baby, baby" vocal improv (similar to "Babe I'm Gonna Leave You") at the 6:13 and 6:28 marks, to be precise.

- "Absolution Blues": Good/solid riffery supplied by Page.

- "Whisper a Prayer for the Dying": Starts sort of similar to "Take Me for a Little While," as it also contains a dark undercurrent musically – before Coverdale goes full-on Plant vocally. Also of note: a string bit that sounds like it was played on a Casio keyboard at the 2:47 mark, which proves to be a bit

125 LED CLONES

of a downer (and those dreaded canon drums... *yeesh*).

But even if you're able to overlook my musical criticisms, what really proved detrimental – and makes the album sound quite dated – was that the duo failed to pay any attention to the studio productions that bands such as Nirvana, Pearl Jam, and Soundgarden had embraced. Which interestingly, both Coverdale and Page helped trailblaze back in the early '70s with their respective bands at the time. And when I spoke to renowned grunge producer Jack Endino (who worked on the first releases by Nirvana and Soundgarden) for my 2015 book, *Survival of the Fittest: Heavy Metal in the 1990's*, he singled out this LP when I asked him about the Led Clones craze of the '80s...despite it being released well into the '90s.

"They were playing '80s production aesthetic to...they were getting part of it, but not all of it. The production thing killed it. If you want the worst example of that, there's the *Coverdale Page* record, that Jimmy Page made with David Coverdale. It's a horrible production. There might have been some good songs on it, but the production just destroyed it, because it was '80s production and it was hideous. A thin little guitar tone, giant drums, horrible vocal tone. It was just a complete embarrassment. Whereas if [Page] had made that record with David Coverdale in 1974, it might have actually been an interesting sounding record – with '1974 production.' It still would have been David Coverdale – who is hard to take – but it wouldn't have had that hideous...I mean, come on, [Deep Purple's] *Burn* is a good record. You've got to give it up for *Burn*. I hate David Coverdale, but *Burn* was a good Deep Purple album! Even if it was the only good Deep Purple that David Coverdale was on, it's still a pretty good record."

Then, when I pointed out the little tidbit to Endino that the album was from 1993 rather than the previous decade, he was flabbergasted. "Wow! That was pretty late in the game. That was like a last-gasp of '80s production, which was sad, because at that point, they should have done it with me. Now you know, in 1995, I was in the studio with Bruce Dickinson [resulting in Dickinson's 1996 solo album, *Skunkworks*]. Who basically was like, 'I don't want to make a record that sounds like this – I like the shit that you're doing! The stuff you're doing sounds like the stuff I grew up on.' And then I realized he was only six months younger than I was and we both grew up listening to the same records."

"And he was like, 'That's what I want to make. I want to make a record that sounds like those great hard rock records from the '70s.' That's kind of what Iron Maiden always wanted to do. And I was like, 'Yeah, I'm there! I'll do that.' So that was interesting to me, like, 'OK, here's an '80s metal guy that wants to make a record that sounds...he likes '90s grunge, he likes the classic stuff. Y'know, he likes King's X, he likes Soundgarden, he likes Jane's Addiction, he likes all this stuff, but he doesn't want to make a record that sounds like *Coverdale Page*. [Laughs] It didn't do my career any good, but it was an interesting experience."

When I asked some of the gentlemen interviewed for this book for some feedback concerning *Coverdale Page*, it varied from the unimpressed, courtesy of Rik Emmett: "That to me smells of John Kalodner saying, 'Hey! Let's do a supergroup project!' And Jimmy goes, 'Well...*OK*. If you're going to throw that much money in my face, I'll give it a run'." But then, there were others who quite fancied it, such as Eddie Trunk: "I liked it a lot. I understand the Zeppelin comparison, but again, how are you going to level that comparison in a negative way to the architect of Led Zeppelin being in the band? If anybody is going to have the

127 LED CLONES

right to do a record that sounds like Led Zeppelin – *it's Jimmy Page*."

"And there was a reason why he got Coverdale – he felt that that was going to work for him, and he wanted to go for that. And I also loved the production. I also loved the drums – which are Denny Carmassi, who played in Montrose and Heart. I think Denny Carmassi is one of the great, unheralded drummers out there. I love his playing. And he very much gets a Bonham vibe – that's not an insult, that's a compliment. So, when you look at how that thing was put together and the people that played on it, and the architect is Jimmy Page, of course it's going to be that."

And it turns out Badlands' Greg Chaisson had similar feelings as Trunk concerning the album. "I actually liked it. I thought the songs were good. Denny Carmassi played great drums on there and kind of had a Bonham feel anyway – even back to his Montrose days. I thought the songs were pretty good. As a matter of fact, the first time I heard it on the radio, I thought, 'What Whitesnake song is this?' But I couldn't tell you what the songs are on it. I thought it was a more complete album than any Whitesnake album – my problem with Whitesnake was always that there would be two or three good songs, and then the rest of it I really didn't connect with."

"And when you're listening to Zeppelin, because it's so varied and Jimmy Page never tried to be a shredder, so he had to be really inventive in how he did stuff, it could carry your interest from song to song to song. I never really felt that with Whitesnake. I thought the players were great, two or three songs a record…and they're certainly not the only band like that. But I thought the *Coverdale Page* record was as close to a Zeppelin sort of thing from a songwriting perspective. I thought it was good – I might be in the minority on that. I think it's Coverdale's best work – go figure."

Me? My thoughts lay somewhere between Emmett's and Trunk/Chaisson's – unlike certain Whitesnake LP's (especially their self-titled and *Slip of the Tongue* offerings), *Coverdale Page* was a much more consistent listen from front to back material-wise. And after all the not-so-nice things I've heard said about it over the years, it wasn't nearly as awful as I thought it would be. In fact, if a few foul ups could have been avoided/corrected (namely, the '80s-esque production, the parts where Coverdale pulls a "Still of the Night" and replicates Plant vocally, and of course, rhyming "promised land" with "understand"), the album would have improved tremendously. In fact, even as it is now, warts and all, I strongly feel that *Coverdale Page* is the sort of album that most Zep fans wanted and expected from a former member to deliver post-1980…and in 1993, *one finally delivered it*.

And the album performed jolly good on the charts, as it peaked at #5 on the *Billboard 200* (again, an impressive feat as this was the height of "grunge mania") and #4 in the UK, plus earning platinum certification Stateside and silver certification across the pond. In fact, in a review for *Kerrang!* upon the album's release, writer Jon Hotten seemed to enjoy the album (giving it a 4 out of 5 review), and stating, "*Coverdale Page* is an exercise in corporate rock. How could it be anything else? Yes, it sounds like Led Zeppelin. Yes, it sounds like Whitesnake, who sounded like Led Zeppelin anyway. These songs are epic blues extravaganzas; occasionally crass, sometimes dated, but most often majestic."

However, the Coverdale Page project proved to be a "one and done" proposition – no world tour would be launched (only a handful of Japanese dates in December '93) and no follow-up issued. Although, those dates did see the

129 LED CLONES

duo perform tunes from the album, as well as classics from both Zep and the 'snake (watching YouTube footage of Page swallowing his pride and performing "Still of the Night" feels like you're transported into some "gone wrong" alternate universe).

During an interview from 2021, Coverdale gave his side of the story as to why we did not hear more from Coverdale Page. "I was very excited. Jimmy and I worked very well creatively, as you can hear, and we had another four or five songs which were unmixed. And I said, 'Jimmy, I've got all these other ideas. Let's just do a *Coverdale Page II* or let's make a double album.' And sadly, his manager at the time talked him out of it, which was infuriating."

"However, some of those songs that I had to present to Jimmy are on the *Restless Heart* record [credited to David Coverdale & Whitesnake] – two of 'em. It was 'Take Me Back Again' and 'Woman Trouble Blues.' Those were originally ideas for Jimmy and I, had we made a second album. But in 2023, it's the 30th anniversary, so look for something special. It's gonna be a lot of fun." Some hoped the "fun" Coverdale mentioned would be a box set, or even a reunion LP or live performances from the duo. However, aside from *Coverdale Page* being reissued on vinyl in Japan that year, nothing else was released nor performed to celebrate its 30th birthday.

Truth be told, probably the *real* reason why Page jumped ship from Coverdale was because of an enticing offer he received from a former Zep mate around this time. With *MTV's Unplugged* being at the height of its popularity in the early to mid '90s (and many artists who appeared on it scoring major hits when issuing their performance as an album), Robert Plant was asked to appear on an episode as a solo artist. However, he would instead opt to ring up Page. And as a result, the highly successful "Page and Plant" project was born.

"I would have been incredibly facetious if I thought I could have carried any thread of the Zeppelin history on my own shoulders outside of a live gig, there and then on the spot, doing a version of 'Living Loving Maid' that sounded like the Knickerbockers," Plant would admit. "And the idea of my doing a whole lot of solo stuff…well, I knew that that's not exactly what everybody would've wanted either – however proud I am of all those songs. It was obvious that I could either say, 'Well, fuck off, I don't like MTV anyway. You don't play me as a rule because I'm too old, so why start worrying about me now?' or I could think about how to team up with the one bloke who knew where I was coming from and see if we couldn't go ahead."

However, Plant admitted some trepidation concerning approaching Page, to see if he'd be interested in working together once more. "My only problem approaching Jimmy, was that we'd never, ever had a conversation in fourteen years about the future together. We'd been bundled into these compromising, well-meaning situations – the charity shows, stuff like that – where there was no preamble, just a conversation on the phone or a conversation between other parties. It's ridiculous how we really didn't even know each other."

But the singer needn't have fretted, as Page was on board. "The MTV thing really was a catalyst, because it gave Robert time to think about things and to get in contact," the guitarist once said. "And when we did, it really was the first time we had a chance to think about the future constructively. To kick it around, see how to do it, how not to do it. It also gave us a chance to write again, to see whether we'd still got that creative spark. And that was happening from Day One."

However, to separate the project from being simply

131 LED CLONES

looked at as a "Led Zeppelin reunion," a decision was made to not include John Paul Jones. "I've read what they've had to say, that they wanted to do a separate project, whatever," Jones said at the time. "I just thought I should have been informed about it. To find out about it in the papers was a bit odd."

As a result, the duo spent a chunk of 1994 rehearsing and writing – with a few numbers featuring a Middle Eastern orchestra for extra pizzazz (with guitarist Porl Thompson, bassist Charlie Jones, and drummer Michael Lee joining in the fun). The end result would be an hour-and-a-half long MTV special which was recorded in August, entitled *Unledded*. Premiered on the channel on October 14th, it would also be issued as an album and DVD entitled *No Quarter: Jimmy Page and Robert Plant Unledded*, which would peak at #4 on the *Billboard 200* (#7 in the UK), and led to a world tour the following year.

Comprised of reworked Zep tunes alongside a handful of new compositions, the top standouts of the entire set are the ones in which the aforementioned Middle Eastern strings (and percussion) are added: "Friends" and "Four Sticks." Of the newly-penned tunes, "Yallah" certainly stands out – not so much because the song itself is all that memorable, but for its lo-fi-esque production, which proves to the perfect antidote to the "over-production" of *Coverdale Page*. Other standouts include a simply outstanding rendition of "Since I've Been Loving You," as well as "Battle of Evermore," which features singer Najma Akhtar doing an exceptional job taking the place of the late Sandy Denny to duet with Plant (and again, the added string and percussion serving as a great addition).

While some of the renditions don't exactly work ("Nobody's Fault But Mine" just kind of meanders along, while "No Quarter" featuring Page's guitar in place of Jones' organ is simply a great big *no-no*), you have to tip your cap to the duo for not taking the easy way out – but rather, trying new/unique approaches to classic material. Also, the duo was solely listed as the project's producer. The end result? The most organic/live sound (finally!) that any Zep member had achieved since the days when Bonzo was still bashing.

However, the same could not be said when the duo issued a proper studio album of all-new material four years later, with the arrival of *Walking into Clarksdale*. When it became known that the duo was recording with Steve Albini (who was best known for his outstanding production work with the likes of such alt-rockers as the Pixies, Nirvana, and PJ Harvey), it certainly appeared to be a promising proposition. However, when the twelve track offering was finally issued on April 20, 1998, it was a bit of a dud – as it sounded as though the duo was merely going through the motions. Not entirely awful however (better than the majority of the solo offerings by Zep members), but there is simply no comparison between the inspired performances included on *No Quarter* than the ones here. In fact, the handful of original tunes included on *No Quarter* proved to be more interesting and more lively than the ones heard on *Walking into Clarksdale*.

Also around the "Page Plant era," their former band was inducted into the Rock and Roll Hall of Fame on January 12, 1995 at the Waldorf Astoria in NYC. Welcomed in by Aerosmith's Steven Tyler and Joe Perry, the most memorable part of the members' speech portion was when John Paul Jones thanked "his friends" for "finally remembering my phone number" (the expression on Robert Plant's face immediately afterwards…*priceless*). As is the case with these induction ceremonies, a "jam session" occurs after the inductees are finished pontificating – and in Zep's case, four songs were performed alongside Tyler and Perry,

133 LED CLONES

with Jason Bonham on drums (covers of "Train Kept A-Rollin'," "Bring It on Home," "Long Distance Call," and "Baby, Please Don't Go"), plus a mini-set closing rendition of "When the Levee Breaks," with Neil Young replacing the Aero duo.

But getting back to *Walking into Clarksdale*, it was clear after its touring cycle that Page and Plant had had enough – and split off to work with others. Subsequently, Page would be paired with the Black Crowes (2000's *Live at the Greek*), and Plant eventually collaborated with Alison Krauss (2007's *Raising Sand*), among other projects. Jones also got back in the swing of things – with the short-lived supergroup, Them Crooked Vultures, which included Queens of the Stone Age's Josh Homme on vocals/guitar and Nirvana/Foo Fighters' Dave Grohl on drums (resulting in 2009's self-titled offering).

With the 20th century winding down, if you were to take a look at what was popular rock and pop-wise on the charts and airwaves (gangsta rap, nu metal, boy bands, etc.), it seemed as if the era of Led Clones may finally be approaching extinction. Little did we know, it would be reaching a whole new level in just a few years.

CHAPTER IX
THE 21ST CENTURY

Right at the dawn of the 21st century, a handful of indie rock bands (actually, make that "indie-turned-major label" rock bands) began making their presence felt on the charts and in the media. Namely, the Strokes and the White Stripes. While the Strokes seemed to have more in common musically with certain first-wave CBGB's bands (Television and Richard Hell and the Voidoids), the White Stripes had certainly studied their garage rock, and, Led Zeppelin records. Led by singer/guitarist Jack White, there has been quite a lot of chatter over the years concerning the similarity between White's and Page's guitar riffery.

But really, to White's credit, if there is any Zep in his style, it's similar to the previous disciples who got it right – using it as a starting point or inspiration (I bet you know what I'm about to say), and then putting his own unique spin on it. And in the process, penned one of the greatest – and most instantly recognizable – riffs of all-time, "Seven Nation Army." And if you really must know a few White riffs that may contain a spread of Led, it turns out that his work *outside* of the Stripes may be your best bet – including the riff that kicks in at the 1:12 mark of his solo tune "High Bell Stepper," as well as the tune "Blue Blood Blues" from another project he has been spotted in, the Dead Weather.

And White once admitted how much Zeppelin was an inspiration, and how their discography is a much-needed antidote to all the software-perfected music of the modern age. "That's the main thing to rebel against right now – over-production, too much technology, overthinking. It's a spoiled mentality; everything is too easy. If you want to record a song, you can buy Pro Tools and record four hundred guitar tracks. That leads to overthinking, which kills any spontaneity and the humanity of the performance. What was interesting about Led Zeppelin was how well they were able to update and capture the essence of the scary part of the blues. A great Zeppelin track is every bit as intense and spontaneous as a Blind Willie Johnson recording." Also worth noting was when White joined Page and U2's The Edge for a chat about guitar for the 2008 documentary, *It Might Get Loud*.

But really, the first of these bands to unashamedly display their love of Zeppelin – and prominently feature it in their music – was a group of rockers from the land down under, Wolfmother. Hailing from Sydney, Australia, and led by curly-afroed singer/guitarist Andrew Stockdale, the group's self-titled debut arrived in 2005 and immediately caused a stir with Stockdale's Plant-like vocals and Page-esque high cholesterol riffs that seemed to be equally modeled after Zeppelin and Sabbath. But again, unlike the Led Clones of the '80s…no need to repeat this point again. And also, props have to be appropriated for the awesomely mammoth, thick, and fuzzed-out sonics cooked up by producer D. Sardy on the debut by W. Mother.

Probably their most Led-like ditty was "Woman," which Stockdale once explained to me what its lyrical inspiration was. "I lived in Sydney, and when I came up with those lyrics for 'Woman,' I was 27. And look, I should say my girlfriend, shouldn't I? [Laughs] Yeah, yeah, it was because of my girlfriend! I think it was an overall impression of living in this beautiful city in the harbor." And the album that "Woman" hails from contained a healthy helping of memorable guitar bits (including the nearly-equally as awesome "Joker and the Thief," which at the time of this book's writing, is a favorite to be blasted at pro hockey games in North America).

"What I am good at is riffs," Stockdale also pointed

out during our chat. "I'll pick up an electric guitar, pick up a bass, and I just have this gut instinct for riffs. I can't explain it, but it's a gut instinct, just really pure, from your being. When I'm playing riffs, I don't like anything fluffy, frilly, weak...there's nothing worse than a weak riff. A weak, flimsy, predictable riff. A riff has to sound familiar, but you've never heard it before. It's like an old friend that you've never met before. Like a kindred spirit that just appears, and you go, 'Yeah! That's it, man! That sticks'!"

Additionally, he offered a few other helpful pointers concerning if a riff is a keeper…or a stinker. "And there's a degree of authenticity to it. You can't overthink it, you can't be like a musical virtuoso, you can't be pretentious, you can't be overly intelligent about it. You've got to transcend all of that control, like you're in personal control. People talk about 'mojo' or 'vibe' or 'juju' – you have to try to get all these elements together, where it's just free and flowing and you're in a sweet spot, and you've got to stay in that sweet spot as long as you can."

Another reason why Wolfmother's self-titled offering succeeds is because like Zeppelin's debut, it was recorded rather quickly. "Everything has to happen quickly: the drums are set up, the guitars are set up, the bass is set up. It's just that you want all that technological stuff to be secondary, and stay out of your way, because you've got to capture the excitement of the track and the intent, the expression, of who you are. The good vibes. You really want to capture the purest emotions coming through, and if you stuff around with mics and walking in and out of the session, and someone comes in, it all gets diluted down and all gets kind of lost. You've got to move quickly and create the best scenario where you can allow it all to happen."

And who could forget the time Stockdale was asked to choose between Sabbath and Zeppelin? "I think I'd go

137 LED CLONES

with Zeppelin, mainly because they've got a more diverse spectrum," he reasoned. "They've got the blues influence, folk, abstract jams, straight balls-to-the-wall rock & roll, ballads. And I do like the sound of all of their albums. Whereas I feel like with Sabbath, the first album was great, but it seems like it got a bit glitzy, a bit too metal, and the lyrical content seemed to be milking the whole sorcerer vibe – death and destruction. After two albums, I can't really listen to that much more of it. I still think it's fantastic, though. I still really enjoy Sabbath in small doses." And on November 14, 2006, Stockdale was able to properly pay tribute to his heroes, when Wolfmother performed "Communication Breakdown" – in front of Jimmy Page! – on the evening that Zeppelin was being inducted into the UK Music Hall of Fame.

And a little over a year after Zep's induction, their three surviving member (plus Jason Bonham) performed what will probably be the group's final full-length concert ever, as the headliner of the Ahmet Ertegun Tribute Concert held at the O2 Arena in London, on December 10, 2007. A solid performance from start to finish (and a zillion times better than either of their two flaccid '80s mini-set reunions), the performance is probably most cherished by long-time fans for the fact that two previously never performed live songs were included – "Ramble On" and "For Your Life."

And in 2012, the full-length O2 performance was issued as a DVD, CD, and vinyl, under the title of *Celebration Day*. Supposedly afterwards, Page, Jones, and Bonham had the hankering to continue…but Plant did not. Hence, a failed attempt at soldiering on with another singer (Aerosmith's Steven Tyler and Alter Bridge's Myles Kennedy supposedly both tried out, while a rumor concerning Soundgarden's Chris Cornell also being considered turned out to be mere hogwash). Wisely, a decision was ultimately made to not attempt to carry on without Plant.

Once more, the one-off reunion seemed to only further increase the arrival of further Zep disciples – including an outfit that appeared on the scene around this time, Rival Sons. Hailing from Long Beach, California, the lads have certainly been known to musically travel over the hills and far away from time to time – especially in the big riffs provided by guitarist Scott Holiday. Case in point, the tune "Tell Me Something" – which served as the album opener on their 2009 full-length debut, *Before the Fire*.

And the guitarist – who is quite distinguishable with his noteworthy facial hair – has voiced his approval of Zeppelin in the press over the years. Such as the time he explained how he first discovered them and their influence. "Growing up in a rock 'n' roll family and having friends that did as well, I noticed every family had a favorite band from those that qualified as the 'Royalty of Rock' – a main band of worship, if you will. We all appreciated most if not ALL the of 'royalty of rock' bands: Beatles, Stones, Floyd, Queen, Zeppelin, etc."

"But if you grew up in a real rock n' roll household, there was always a primary focal point band that a family really believed in or thought (ex: like your dad being a Chevy OR Ford guy) were the be-all-end-all BEST. For my family this band was Led Zeppelin. So when you hear their influence in my music, just understand. I was brainwashed. My family programmed these lullabies into my memories from birth. And they lasted well into my 20's."

Another band that first surfaced early in the 21st century that would eventually publicly display their affection of the Zeppers was the most non-hard rocking of the bunch – as they leaned more towards the poppier side of things. And that band would be the rather plainly-named

139 LED CLONES

Train. Led by a dashing-looking singer by the name of Pat Monahan, the San Fran band is best known for such schmaltzy soft rock mega-hits as "Drops of Jupiter (Tell Me)" (or now that I think about it, perhaps simply "early '70s Elton John/Bernie Taupin knock-off" is a kinder, more fitting description of the tune). But the first sign of their affection for Zep was when they covered "Ramble On" during an appearance on *The Howard Stern Show* in 2001.

And similar to what Triumph's Rik Emmett admitted earlier in this book, Monahan paid his dues singing the blues...I mean, *Zep tunes* in bars before hitting it big. "I was in a cover band that did three sets a night, and then the last set was the Zeppelin set. That's when everybody would show up to see us, and we never got it through our thick heads that maybe we should just do all Led Zeppelin and then they could have shown up earlier."

But it was in 2016 that the group would decide to go whole hog into their appreciation of the Leds, when they issued the album *Train Does Led Zeppelin II*. Never before has there been a much truer album title concerning what contents lurked within – a faithful, song-by-song rendition of one of the greatest rock albums ever issued (and perhaps the greatest example of avoiding the dreaded "sophomore slump").

And just how/why did Train cover *Zep II*? "When we learned Led Zeppelin covers in the past, the three that we would do normally, two of them were off this record – 'What Is and What Should Never Be' and 'Ramble On,'" the singer once confessed [and for those keeping score at home, the third Zep number they'd tackle was not off *II*, but rather, *IV*, "Going to California"]. "We were just like, 'Hey, we're two [songs] in on a nine song album, let's just learn the rest.'"

It turns out that due to technological advancements of modern times, figuring out how to replicate such a landmark album was easier than ever. "We went in and really learned, the best that we could, all of the things that they did," the singer recalled about the release of *TDLZII*. "In fact, we even went to YouTube and listened to lone vocals that we could find. It was pretty interesting."

But that said, the singer admitted it wasn't simply an easy stroll through Evermore. "Every part of it was challenging. I think that my band did an incredible job, I mean, even getting tones and everything right. The challenge is just to do it and then to try to cut vocals and have enough in me to do several takes at a time. I don't know how [Robert Plant] did it – and he's so great."

Now, with all the backstory of how Train came to cover the album…how exactly did it all add up when actually listened to? First the good – performance-wise from a vocal and guitar perspective (with guitars provided by Luis Maldonado and Jerry Becker), it was certainly done in an admirable manner. And sonically, it was not too shabby, either – that is, except for the tight drum sound (courtesy of Drew Shoals) totally lacks the power and spaciousness that the great Bonzo created on the original recording.

Now, the bad – was this release *really* necessary? I mean, it's one thing perhaps experiencing this performed live…but who in their right mind would choose listening to this rather than the real McCoy? While it was certainly a nice gesture paying tribute to Zeppelin, it's a note-for-note faithful reproduction of the original (even the bloody drum solo in "Moby Dick"). Which leads to the obvious question or thought – what's the difference between this and an expert karaoke or tribute band rendition?

And now, we are at the point of the book that we will discuss a band that was so Zep-like, that they caused an uproar not seen/heard since the days of when Kingdom Come enjoyed their 15 minutes (months?) of fame. And that

141 LED CLONES

lucky band would be, of course, Greta Van Fleet. The Frankenmuth, Michigan (no, I never heard of that town, either) natives' main shtick when they first burst onto the scene was just how young the members were – either late teenaged or in their early twenties, with three of the band being brothers (singer Josh and guitarist Jake Kiszka are twins, and bassist Sam). First issuing a pair of EP's in 2017 (*Black Smoke Rising* and *From the Fires*) before going the full-length route (2018's *Anthem of the Peaceful Army*, 2021's *The Battle of Garden's Gate*, and 2023's *Starcatcher*), the band at first opted to go the "I don't know what you're talking about" route when it came to their music coming in such close contact with Zeppelin.

For example, that time in 2017 when I interviewed young Jake for *BraveWords* and asked about the band's influences. His reply didn't include a single peep about their most obvious influence. "We all share some influences – especially when it comes to the realm of blues. But we all have very varying influences and quite eclectic when it comes down to it. Personally, some of my influences – because I'm a guitar player – are Elmore James, Muddy Waters, Jimi Hendrix, Pete Townshend, and Robby Krieger."

And six years later, he shared a similar stance. "As for Led Zeppelin – we weren't listening to rock music growing up; that happened in high school. So we're talking about the originations of the genres that we now consider to be folk music, like Woody Guthrie and Bob Dylan. We had Alan Lomax records laying around. It was roots of the Great American South and the Blue Hills – bluegrass music and banjo playing."

However, in 2019, Josh was willing to come clean, when the subject of Zeppelin's influence on GVF came up during a chat with *Rolling Stone*, and he admitted,

"Obviously we hear the similarity. That's one of the influences of ours. But at this point it's like, 'Okay, we've acknowledged that. Let's move on'."

Still, some were clearly not ready to simply "move on," as the group continued to take their lumps and bumps in the press – such as the time *Anthem of the Peaceful Army* received a puny 1.6 (out of 10) rating in an album review by Jeremy D. Lawson for *Pitchfork*. And during the scathing review, Lawson declared "The debut from the young Michigan rock band is stiff, hackneyed, overly precious retro-fetishism."

And his verbal assault didn't end there, as he continued by venting, "Greta Van Fleet sound like they did weed exactly once, called the cops, and tried to record a Led Zeppelin album before they arrested themselves," before following it up with, "They make music that sounds exactly like Led Zeppelin and demand very little other than forgetting how good Led Zeppelin often were." And finally, going for the knockout blow with "And at least Zeppelin knew to separate their sweet-lady-I'm-horny songs from their howling-about-literary-fantasy songs."

There was also a time in which the foremost expert on the topic – Robert Plant – shared his opinion, by saying, "There is a band in Detroit called Greta Van Fleet – *they are Led Zeppelin I*. The kid looks like he's been dropped out of like…a beautiful little singer. I hate him! He borrowed it from somebody I know very well. But what are you going to do?"

Also, another gentleman who has had to endure his share of Zep comparisons, Jack White, also shared his stance on GVF – and even provided some constructive criticism. "They're three Polish brothers from Frankenmuth, Michigan – I thought that was a joke! But it's exciting to see young people play rock & roll, no doubt about it. That guy has a very cool voice. The more he makes it his own, the better. People used to say, when I first came out, 'He sounds like Robert Plant.' If you keep pushing forward, that shit goes away."

Add to it a time in the past where Anthrax drummer Charlie Benante said, "They're young kids, and I think what you're hearing is they're very impressionable and taking certain elements of Led Zeppelin and kind of putting it into this filter, and this is what they came out with. Some of the things are reminiscent of a Zeppelin tune, as well. But I thought they did it very well. And it sucks when you read things like, 'They don't sound like Zeppelin.' It's like, 'Come on guys...*stop*'."

And lastly, how about we let Eddie Trunk share his thoughts on this hot topic? "Zeppelin to this day, to some degree, is *still* the blueprint – look no further than the success of Greta Van Fleet. Who, I think may be the most blatant-ever Zeppelin sounding band, and who have done the best of all these bands that we're talking about for the most part. I mean, in terms of longevity and building into an arena act and building a big following – I find that one immensely interesting."

Now that we've heard from others concerning what their "Greta thoughts" are, ever wonder what Greg Prato thinks of this seemingly controversial band? If so, you're now in luck. Although there is no denying there is a distinct Zep quality to tunes such as "Highway Tune" and "Safari Song" (most obvious by Joshua K's Plant-y vocals and Jake K's Page-y riffing), I don't find them nearly as offensive nor comical as say, Kingdom Come's "Get It On" or Whitesnake's "Still of the Night." Why? A few reasons.

First off, from what I've heard from the band, there are no clear moments of where the young chaps directly lifted riffs from "Black Dog" or "Kashmir" (like the two aforementioned '80s wrongdoers did)…although the drum opening of "Sacred the Thread" is too close to "When the Levee Breaks" for my liking. Secondly, one of my favorite rock bands of all-time is Rush. And if we are to judge Rush solely by their first album, they were *highly* derivative of Zeppelin. In case you forget how much, I suggest you take a quick listen to "Finding My Way" right now to see what I mean (go ahead, I'll still be here when you return). Also, while we're on the topic of Rush, there are GVF tunes in which Josh's vocals sound more like '70s era *Geddy Lee* than *Robert Plant* (the tunes "Black Smoke Rising" and "When the Curtain Falls," in particular).

Thirdly, judging from their first few releases, GVF does not seem like a one-trick pony – as evidenced by such tunes as the piano ballad "Light My Love," or the fact that some of their tunes, such as "You're the One," could have been a hit power ballad back in the '80s. Especially, if you replaced the organ with a Casio, swapped producers Marlon Young, Al Sutton, and Herschel Boone with either Tom Werman, Beau Hill, or Spencer Proffer, and also, issued an accompanying music video shot partly in black and white and partly in color, that focused on the rigors of life on the road and missing your honey. Now, all that said, would I spin a GVF LP as opposed to a Zeppelin classic during my cherished daily music listening schedule? *Absolutely not.* But then again, I'm also quite a few miles out of GVF's age demographic…

And the last early 21st century Zep-derived band we will tackle is LA's own Dirty Honey. And the part of the band that was reeked most of Led were some of the riffs provided by guitarist John Notto – particularly the bit contained at the 1:01 mark of the tune "Rolling 7s," off their self-titled EP from 2019. And wouldn't you know it, Notto once admitted that it was a certain Zeppelin tune that was the very first he learned as a student of the six-string.

"'Stairway to Heaven' was the first song that I really took lessons from a guy and had him show it to me, over the course of many lessons, and get it all the way, because even though it's long, it's really not super complicated. It's just got a lot of parts, until you get to the guitar solo, of course. But, just had a knack for it early on, and I was always into old music from the baby boomer generation. So I, yeah, from my mom's record collection and stuff. So I just gravitated to that stuff."

And of course, there were others around this time that also liked their Led, including the Black Keys (the tune "Little Black Submarines"), the Vintage Caravan ("Midnight Meditation" and "Expand Your Mind"), Royal Blood ("Little Monster"), plus Earthless ("Black Heaven" manages to merge "Good Times Bad Times" and "Whole Lotta Love" together in the same bloody riff!), among others.

Another band of the era that contains some Zep moments is one featuring former Badlands bassist Greg Chaisson, entitled Atomic Kings – who issued a self-titled album in 2023. And musically, it sounds like they picked up where Badlands left off. "The Atomic Kings definitely has a certain Zeppelin vibe, along with a lot of other things – not a clone of anything," explains Chaisson.

"But much like Badlands, we still wear our influences on our sleeve. If there's something that we like about something and it has a certain Zeppelin feel or a Humble Pie feel or a Mott the Hoople feel, we'll explore it and expand on it. 'I Got Mine' and 'Take My Hand' have a certain Zeppelin feel to it. 'Running Away,' which is sort of our pseudo-ballad – our drummer was playing a drum part and we started writing a song to it, and we got to an impasse, and I said, 'It needs to kind of have a 'Kashmir' sort of feel.' And when we showed up the next time to rehearse, it had a

'Kashmir' feel!"

But before this chapter's last stand, how about a few of the gentlemen interviewed for this book share their opinions about the modern day bands that have a Zep-inian flair to them? "I love Greta Van Fleet," admitted Mark Clarke. "Absolutely love 'em. One of my daughters turned me on to them. They're such Zeppelin fans, but they do their own thing. And it comes naturally. You see the bass player and the drummer live, he doesn't try to play like Bonham or Jonesy. They just do their own thing. But it comes across as Zeppelin. I've loved Greta Van Fleet for a couple of years now, actually."

"Greta Van Fleet I have heard, and went, 'Oh, OK – they're going to school on Zeppelin'," added Rik Emmett. "What will they do with this in four years hence, five years hence? I like it. There are ways that you can approach things, and I don't mind a band that goes, 'Hey, we're going to be like a Led Zeppelin band.' And I go, 'Great…but what are you going to do with it? Are you just going to be a Led Zeppelin band? Or are you going to use that as a foundation to do the things that make you become *an artist*?' So, when a band is young, I try not to rush to judgement. I go, 'OK. See what happens four or five years down the line'."

However, unlike Clarke and Emmett, Alan Niven did not sound very impressed with the Gretas. "Oh God…*stop*. Ask me if I have a Greta Van Fleet album? No. It's just Jason Flom [who signed the band to Republic Records] doing 'Zeppelin paint by the numbers.' That's exactly what that is. And they're a boy band. I mean, what do they stand for? Who are they? What are they writing about? 'Oh, we really know how to knock off Zeppelin's studio sound.' *Boring*."

Greg Chaisson also was willing to make his opinion known. "Greta Van Fleet was the one I was talking about that they have a Zeppelin influence, but the singer is going

147 LED CLONES

out of his way to say, 'No. I never listened to Zeppelin.' It's like, 'Come on, dude. *Get a grip*.' Wolfmother and Big Elf reminded me more of Uriah Heep than I would say Zeppelin, although there are certain aspects of those bands that would kind blur the line a little bit with each other. And then you have bands like Rival Sons that has a certain Zeppelin bent – especially the drum sound. That's a good Bonham drum sound on that. The songs are good, they're not copying Zeppelin but you can definitely hear the Zeppelin influence thing."

"With Dirty Honey I can hear some of the Zeppelin influence. The thing about Greta Van Fleet, Rival Sons, and Dirty Honey is the bass players are really good. And you can definitely hear where there could be a John Paul Jones influence in there – especially the earlier John Paul Jones, where he was really off the chain. If you're listening to 'Lemon Song' and you're listening to all the stuff he's doing, or even on the outro part of 'The Ocean,' you can definitely hear the influence with those guys. Vocally, I know what they're trying to do – at least Dirty Honey and Greta Van Fleet. And I'll tip my hat to them. I think they're both good bands…but if you're going to use Zeppelin as a template, you should own up to it."

And lastly, let's pass the mic to Eddie Trunk. "To me, Greta Van Fleet is the most blatant. I honestly was shocked at the out of the gate interest/excitement/embracing that Greta Van Fleet had. And to me, it was very similar – having worked in radio for over 40 years – to what happened with Kingdom Come. I felt like that first song, 'Highway Tune,' was going to be their 'Get It On' – and then the backlash would probably happen like with all these other bands immediately, and then it would end. But it didn't. They maintained and they held on."

"I gave them initially the benefit of the doubt on it,

because they were so incredibly young when they started. I'm sure they grew up with their dad's records or whatever, and everybody has that influence. So, I'm like, 'Cut them some slack, let's see what happens. When they get a little older maybe they'll find their own way. Maybe they'll evolve out of this and find their own sound.' I haven't listened to them all that much – it kind of escapes me a little bit, what they've become."

"But what I've heard, it still sounds a lot like Zeppelin – a lot of the things they've done. But, to their credit, they have maintained. And they built a great audience. They're certainly good players. And the Zeppelin thing…people don't seem to say it that much about them anymore. And I always have said any young group of musicians in this environment that can break through and be successful in rock, I give credit to. And they certainly have done that."

"Rival Sons – one of my favorite bands of the last 20 years. And yes, the Zeppelin influence is clearly there. But there's something that I find in them, that I think they're still also somewhat on their own trip, doing their own thing. And enough of that is interjected in there – in my opinion. But yes, clearly there's that. But I love those guys. I think Jay Buchanan is one of the best singers we have today. Wolfmother certainly has those big riffs. Andrew's voice certainly belts it out – I like that. I certainly hear it in them."

"Dirty Honey, yes, that's definitely a thing with them and there's that sound. But what people night not know about Dirty Honey is that Marc LaBelle – the singer – used to be in a band that paid tribute to Aerosmith. *Not Zeppelin.* Again, anybody's going to love Zeppelin that's a rock band – but they actually had some pretty different influences in there, as well. But, I'm sure they understand why people say it – the riffs and the vocal are in that world, for sure."

Trunk brings up a good point – why was a band like

149 LED CLONES

Kingdom Come so vilified and their career fleeting, whereas Greta Van Fleet is several top-10 LP's into their career and able to headline arenas and festivals? I couldn't help but ask his thoughts behind why/how this puzzling matter occurred. "I think the radio landscape has changed dramatically now versus the days of Kingdom Come. Today, radio is basically run by two major companies. One or two people dictate what's played or not. So, if you are anointed as 'cool' and 'playable,' it sticks. Back in the '80s, radio was more independent-minded. And I think programmers after the buzz of 'Get It On' expired, looked at the band as more of almost a novelty and moved off of them quick. Programmers don't have that autonomy today."

So, there you have it – we're all caught up to date (at least when this book was released) concerning the artists who have borrowed a guitar lick, beat, bassline, vocalization, lyric, sonic-approximation, or look, from Led Zeppelin. Will there be more to arrive in the future? I'd like to slightly modify a famous proverb: "Nothing is certain except death and taxes…*and each decade's new wave of Led Zeppelin pupils.*"

CHAPTER X
ZEPPELIN CLONED OTHERS?

Judging from some of the quotes in this book, the former members of Led Zeppelin were never shy about voicing their opinions concerning some of the artists they influenced – seemingly more often than not, not in the most glowing of terms, either. However (if I may dig back into my stash of proverbs), this could very well be a case of the pot calling the kettle black. What am I getting at? Let me explain…

Back in the days before you had an endless amount of encyclopedic information at your fingertips (I avoided using the dreaded "*before the internet*" phrase), it was easy to pull the wool over someone's eyes. But it seemed like with each passing year, further accusations were hurled at Led Zeppelin over a bad habit they picked up during their recording career – swiping songs from other artists, not properly crediting them, and claiming them as entirely penned by members of their band.

Was it a case of Zeppelin's record label or management not properly doing their job? Was it a decision by the band members themselves? It's hard to tell, but if you are able to track down early pressings of Zeppelin LP's and take a gander at the vinyl's center rings where the song titles and writer credits are listed, you'll notice that a few are missing names that should certainly be there. To name but a few, "Dazed and Confused" on *Led Zeppelin I* simply listed "Page" as the author…whereas in reality, a chap by the name of Jake Holmes had previously penned a tune of the same name and which contained the same descending guitar line (but different lyrics). Yet, received no credit.

Never mind the fact that the guitar fill 28 seconds into Jimi Hendrix's rendition of "Hey Joe" sounds identical to the main riff in "Whole Lotta Love," but what about the

151 LED CLONES

fact that "Page-Plant-Jones-Bonham" were listed solely as the authors of the tune on early pressings of *Led Zeppelin II*, whereas lyrical bits of the Willie Dixon-penned tune "You Need Love" were clearly plucked and inserted in Zep's classic tune? And what was up with "The Lemon Song" once more listing all four Zep members, without a mention of Chester Burnett (aka, Howlin' Wolf), who penned the tune "Killing Floor," which served as the lyrical basis for Zep's bluesy tune? You want one more glaring example of Zep's dishonest crediting habits? Look no further than "In My Time of Dying" off *Physical Graffiti*, which once again, originally merely listed all four Zeps, with no mention of Blind Willie Johnson, who penned a tune entitled "Jesus Make Up My Dying Bed" way back in 1928, which is a line that Plant clearly sings in the Zep tune.

And truth be told, I was unable to track down an image of the center vinyl ring of the original pressing of *Led Zeppelin IV*, but I wouldn't be surprised if Memphis Minnie was not initially credited for the album's closing tune, "When the Levee Breaks" – a song she co-wrote and recorded with a chap by the name of Kansas Joe McCoy way back yonder in 1929. Or, if her name was indeed properly listed on the record in 1971, it would have been one of the first times that Zeppelin gave credit where credit is due. But either way, where is Mr. McCoy's credit on *Zep IV*?

In case you were wondering, the list goes on and on – with *Rolling Stone* going on to pen an article entitled "Led Zeppelin's 10 Boldest Rip-Offs" in 2016, while a multi-part series on YouTube entitled "Led Zeppelin Plagiarism" proves to be a fascinating listen (as it plays part of the plagiarized song first, followed by Zeppelin's version). And it turns out that Zep's "adoption" of bits from blues artists ran so deep that it even affected Robert Plant's vocal improv in concert. For example, in the version of "Whole Lotta Love" from *The Song Remains the Same,* when he does the "One night I was laying down, I hear my mom and papa talking…" portion, it's a direct lift from John Lee Hooker's "Boogie Chillun" ("One night I was laying down, I heard mom and papa talking, I heard papa tell mama, 'Let that boy boogie woogie'").

Even the middle part of John Bonham's drum solo showcase, "Moby Dick," appears to be closely modeled after a renowned jazz drummer's tune. "I've got a tape somewhere of how he got the idea for 'Moby Dick'," recalled Bonzo's former drum tech, Jeff Ocheltree. "Steve Smith and some other drummers pointed out to me, 'That's kind of a take-off on Max Roach's 'The Drum Also Waltzes'.' Which is a tune that Max wrote" [and included on his 1966 album, *Drums Unlimited*].

And also, let's not forget the striking similarity between the classic drum bit that kicks off Zep's "Rock and Roll" and the opening of Little Richard's "Keep A-Knockin' (But You Can't Come In)" – the latter of which was provided by drummer Charles Connor, and originally released in 1957.

But the most public display of an artist crying foul and accusing Zeppelin of stealing was when a surviving member of the band Spirit, bassist Mark Andes, filed a copyright infringement suit against Zeppelin in May of 2014, due to the supposed musical similarity between "Stairway to Heaven" and the Spirit tune "Taurus" – the latter of which was penned by guitarist Randy California and included on the band's self-titled debut from 1968. And since California had been deceased since 1997, his former bandmate filed the claim.

After years of various rulings and appeals (including all three surviving Zeppelin members having to testify in court), it was determined on March 9, 2020 that Led

153 LED CLONES

Zeppelin did not infringe on the copyright of Spirit's "Taurus." And on October 5th, the Supreme Court of the United States officially ended the copyright dispute. A year afterward, Plant shared his views concerning the "Taurus"/"Stairway to Heaven" saga, when he stated, "There are zillions and zillions of songs that are carrying the same chord progression, so it was very unfortunate, and it was unpleasant for everybody."

And it turns out this was not the first time Zeppelin was brought into court – back in 1987, Willie Dixon reached an out of court settlement with the band, over the fact that their tune "Bring It On Home" was a virtual cover of the song by the same name by Dixon (and covered by Sonny Boy Williamson in 1966), and as mentioned before, the lyrics of another tune he penned, "You Need Love," were pinched for "Whole Lotta Love." As an added part of the settlement, Dixon was solely credited as the composer of "Bring It On Home" on subsequent reissues of *Led Zeppelin II* (whereas previously – you guessed it – Page and Plant were solely credited).

When asked about Zeppelin's penchant for "borrowing" from others, Alan Niven reasoned that "People like Page, the Who, and Keith Richards, who were immersed in black American music of the '40s and '50s, and in some respects, you can say they really did develop that. And there's some respects where Zeppelin just stole it. The interesting aspect is in mentioning Ten Years After and Savoy Brown…and the Kinks. With Dave Davies for example, you're looking at somebody that really brought out perfect fifth chords – playing the root with the fifth note, and the terminology changed later to 'power chord.' And Jimmy did that in spades on *Zeppelin I*."

Also, Eddie Trunk shared his thoughts concerning this sensitive subject. "Most people know that the songs on certainly the first Zeppelin record, half of them were basically just re-writes of blues songs that they loved. Not giving credit or songwriting credit is certainly an issue – and that should certainly be looked at and resolved. And maybe some of it has been. But I think that Zeppelin's acknowledgment of where the blues influenced them and where they took so much stuff...they acknowledged it."

"And the thing about the lawsuit with 'Stairway to Heaven,' I don't know – I've listened to it, I know what they're talking about. But I didn't really feel like there was enough there as far as a lawsuit. I think it was the band Spirit that went after them. It comes down to the amount you're using. Also, is it coincidental? Is it intentional? Of course, they're all going to say it's not by design. But who knows if it really is. So, it's so hard to prove. And then it comes down to how many bars and how reminiscent is it of it. But I felt some of it was valid – certainly with some of the blues guys. And then when it comes down to the thing with Spirit, I think it was probably them just making a run at trying to cash out a little bit."

Lastly, Rik Emmett explained, "Zeppelin themselves got sued by lots of writers that were going...Willie Dixon is going, 'Hey, you stole my song here. You're claiming it as yours. It's not yours.' And then quietly, Zeppelin is going, 'OK, we'll give you a lot of money. We don't want to have to put your name on the album. How much will you take to keep your name out of it?' But there were other instances of, 'No, no. You've got to put my name on there'."

"I was consulted by the CBC – the Canadian equivalent of the BBC – when that lawsuit thing was going down by the lawyer representing the estate of Randy California, because of 'Stairway to Heaven.' They asked me, 'What is your opinion?' I sat down, listened to the things, and go, 'Look, there's no question that Page is using that

155 LED CLONES

progression that Randy California used. But, I can also play you something from a 16th century Italian composer that uses exactly that same progression in a Renaissance piece of music'."

"You can't copyright progressions. And in any case, Jimmy gets to the end of the progression, and he plays this 12-string rhythm part that's not in the other guy's tune *at all*. So, what Jimmy does is he takes his influences, and he takes them to another place. He creates something. We live in a world of mash-ups, and now, it's something different. The integrity of this is something different because it's kind of fresh and kind of new. And pop music has done that all of its life. So, to turn around and say, 'Now I'm going to make fun of somebody that's done that,' and you go, 'Well, *you do it too'*."

Way back in 1988, *Rolling Stone's* David Fricke asked Plant, "What's your opinion of producer Rick Rubin and what he did with the Led Zeppelin sound on the Beastie Boys' album? He seems to be one of the few people trying to take that thing out on a different tangent." Part of Plant's reply? "Maybe he ought to write his own riffs then."

Hmmm…

CHAPTER XI
WHY SO MANY IN THE '80s?

As we've discussed for much of this book, each decade from the '70s onward contained its fair share of artists inspired by Led Zeppelin. But as evidenced by the amount of pages in this book dedicated to the '80s, it was undoubtedly the decade that gave us the most artists who "got the Led out." Which leads to an obvious question... "Why?"

It turns out that I don't think there was one clear-cut reason. But rather, *several*. The most obvious one being that once Zeppelin was put out of commission in the wake of John Bonham's death in 1980, it left an enormous void in the rock world. And with demand for the band seemingly as high as it ever was throughout the decade (especially if you were to judge by the fact that they were still constantly played on rock radio and the large amount of media coverage) – but with the actual band unable to cash in on it with new albums or tours – others quickly moved in with a similar style/approach. Also, if the '80s solo efforts by former Zep members were on par quality-wise with their former band, perhaps it would have satisfied the public's demand a bit more – instead of having to seek out bands that sounded more like Led Zeppelin than its actual former members.

So, that said, you have to wonder if Bonham did not die when he did, would there have been as many Led Clones in the '80s? "No, I don't think it had anything to do with Bonham's passing," said Triumph's Rik Emmett. "I think it had everything to do with the way Lee Abrams and people like that started programming AOR radio. So, the idea of a melodic, heavy rock...and it wasn't *just* Zep. They were obviously the instigators of it, but along had come Styx, Kansas – melodic, progressive, but accessible. Journey had refined – *and defined* – a thing where it was becoming even more melodic and more poppy in terms of the song structures."

"If you look at Zeppelin and go, 'Where did they come from?' They came from Jimmy's riffy, Yardbirds-y, psychedelic, freak out-y kind of stuff. But he also liked British folk. There was a lot of Davey Graham and John Renbourn – that kind of style of fingerpicking and open-tunings. And that was of course right up Robert Plant's alley – he loved all that folky, rootsy music. Robert Plant is almost like a musicologist, in a way. So, the marriage of Plant and Page was this very strong understanding of…and a lot of Americana, blues-rootsy kind of influences. When the other bands started to come into it, now it wasn't so much that. It was much more a question of, 'What will hit radio formats in the guts'?"

Great White's former manager/songwriter, Alan Niven, also was willing to share his opinion on the topic. "Timing. I think a lot of people thought enough time had passed [since Bonham's death] and there is no new Led Zeppelin, and there is no old Led Zeppelin, so…let's be *a* Led Zeppelin. And I think that people thought they could get away with that. And that's why I think exactly why Jason Flom has painted Greta Van Fleet into 'Led Zeppelin boy band lite.' I think it's all about timing. Zeppelin sold a lot of records, Zeppelin sold a lot of tickets. There are people who run businesses – record companies and promoters – who go, 'If we had another Zeppelin, that would make my bank manager really happy'."

And it turns out that Eddie Trunk's reasoning was very similar to mine. "Well, I think it was driven by the fact that Led Zeppelin ended in 1980, and they were – without a doubt – probably the most celebrated/respected hard rock band coming out of the '70s. And influential. I think because Zeppelin got so much radio airplay and were so loved and celebrated, a lot of musicians coming up at the time in the '80s saw a void there. And saw an opportunity to fill that void – and maybe step into it a little bit by coming up with maybe a similar sound."

Another observation I'd like to make public: Beatles and Black Sabbath-influenced bands seem to be much more accepted by the masses (and critics), whereas most Led Zeppelin-influenced bands *were not*. The only reason I can gather is because Led Clones proved to be more irritating and grating than say, the British Invasion or stoner/doom metal bands that obviously use the Fab Four or the Sabs (respectively) as a template for their sounds/approaches.

And while some of the artists discussed in this book have held up musically better than others, it sounds as if Rik Emmett can find value in those who do…and do not. "I liked them all. They're derivative, so if they only had a little bit more originality to them, then as they evolved, they would then become a band that could last. But if you remain derivative…you might get an album or two, but you're not going to stick around. Whereas you see a band like Rush – they were evolving like crazy. They get Neil [Peart] into the band, and they try this 'science fiction' kinda thing for a bit, and then they go, 'OK. We should evolve into our own thing. We should be what we are good at as an ensemble. Let's be more about ourselves."

"The whole thing about integrity is an interesting thing that's obviously going to be a part of your book. Because when you're being derivative, in its early stages, it's critical – you *have to* do it. You have to say, 'Hey, Robert Johnson' or 'Muddy Waters.' It's got to come from somewhere. When I was a kid, I had a Segovia album, and I did a piss-poor job of emulating that. But it was a part of who I became and what I do as a musician. You've got to start *somewhere*. Bar bands, you've got to play cover material.

159 LED CLONES

And it's never going to leave you – it's always going to be a part of what you do. But you have to grow from there."

As discussed and analyzed in chapters eight and nine, Zeppelin's influence on other artists has continued beyond the '80s, and goes right through to the modern day. And I once had the opportunity to ask Jason Bonham (who since 2010 has toured as a Zep tribute band, dubbed "Jason Bonham's Led Zeppelin Evening") why he thinks that the band's music continues to resonate with subsequent generations. His reply?

"As I've gotten older I could still put that music on and it still stands up to anything when you play it – sonically, sound-wise. There's still nothing ever like it, the way it was written. It was written outside the box. I know it was different times then. But the way they were individually as players, how good they were individually and collectively as a band, it was even better."

"It's funny – I was talking to Robert only an hour ago and we were going through some old fun stories. It was just nice to grow up as a part of this. Even though my father is not around, there is a certain calmness that I feel through the music and what people write to me and talk to me about, and the work that dad did for them. I'm very lucky that I get to go and play this great music and have fun with it. And play live – which is what I love, when young people and fans come out to see the show. So thank you, to everybody."

Lastly, the following quote from Eddie Trunk just may have succeeded in summing up the goal of this entire book in two sentences. And also, serves as the perfect parting thought. "You can go '70s, '80s, '90s, 2000's, you're always going to make that line to Zeppelin. It's just a question of, *'How over the top blatant is it'?"*

TOP 50 TUNES

1. Kingdom Come: Get It On
2. Whitesnake: Still of the Night
3. Rush: Finding My Way
4. Rush: Working Man
5. Greta Van Fleet: Highway Tune
6. Bonham: Wait for You
7. Montrose: Rock Candy
8. Billy Squier: Lonely Is the Night
9. Heart: Barracuda
10. Wolfmother: Woman
11. Moxy: Train
12. Fastway: Say What You Will
13. Michael White: Psychometry
14. Zebra: Tell Me What You Want
15. Great White: Rock Me
16. Aerosmith: Round and Round
17. ZZ Top: Precious and Grace
18. Deep Purple: Perfect Strangers
19. Alice Cooper: It's Hot Tonight
20. Kiss: Larger Than Life
21. Queen: Liar
22. Badlands: Winter's Call
23. Soundgarden: Incessant Mace
24. Nirvana: Aero Zeppelin
25. Lenny Kravitz: Always on the Run
26. Blind Melon: Seed to a Tree
27. Stone Temple Pilots: Sin
28. White Stripes: Icky Thump
29. Rival Sons: Tell Me Something
30. Dirty Honey: Rolling 7s
31. Dixie Dregs: Bloodsucking Leeches
32. Blue Murder: Valley of the Kings
33. Van Halen: Poundcake

161 LED CLONES

34. The Cult: Soul Asylum
35. Red Hot Chili Peppers: Suck My Kiss
36. Earthless: Black Heaven
37. Masters of Reality: VHV
38. Jane's Addiction: Pigs in Zen
39. Primus: Shake Hands With Beef
40. Stone Roses: Love Spreads
41. Bad Company: Feel Like Makin' Love
42. Kansas: Carry on Wayward Son
43. Tommy Bolin: Shake the Devil
44. T. Rex: 20th Century Boy
45. Triumph: Be My Lover
46. Funkadelic: Alice in My Fantasies
47. Mother Love Bone: Heartshine
48. Slaughter: Fly to the Angels
49. Beastie Boys: Rhymin' & Stealin'
50. Gary Moore (w/ Ozzy Osbourne): Led Clones

SOURCES

Chapter I: What Made Led Zeppelin So Darn Influential?

Mendelsohn: "It would seem…their collective attention." (*Rolling Stone* – March 15, 1969), Lester Bangs: ""Unfortunately, precious little…to Iggy Stooge." (*Rolling Stone* – November 26, 1970, Miller: "Naturally, *Graffiti* is…succumb to monotony." (*Rolling Stone* – March 27, 1975)**,** Plant: "Bonzo used to…your ass out." (*Kerrang!* – March 24, 1990), Page: "A riff ought…and over again." (*Rolling Stone* – December 6, 2012)

Chapter II: The '70s

Lifeson: "In the beginning…that we have." (*Louder Sound* – February 8, 2024), Lee: "As soon as…that drum sound!" (*My Effin' Life* book – 2023), Lee: "Plant's extreme vocal…our new paradigm." (*My Effin' Life* book – 2023), Lee: "Zeppelin challenged the…just plain wimpy." (*My Effin' Life* book – 2023), Lee: "Musicians talk about…was that profound." (*CBC News: The National* – November 12, 2023), Lifeson: "We were three…in our underwear." (interview with author – August 3, 2024), Halper: "I was up…we get one'?" (*Rush: Beyond the Lighted Stage* documentary – 2010), Lifeson: "'Working Man' was…Working kids, indeed!" (*The 100 Greatest Songs of Heavy Metal* eBook – 2023), Lee: "There are so…all-around musical talent." (*Rolling Stone* – December 4, 2019), Emmett: "I think the…you could make." (interview with author – August 7, 2024), Hagar: "The first Montrose…to a hundred." (*Rolling Stone* – March 6, 2012), Hagar: "I went and…because of Ronnie." (*Rolling Stone* – March 6, 2012), Hagar: "We made one…Montrose' I saw." (*Rolling Stone* – March 6, 2012), Wilson: "There were no…at the time." (*Guitar World* – June 7, 2024), Wilson: "We'd been opening…hard to recreate." (*Loudwire* – March 5, 2019), Wilson: "Jimmy Page came…Keep working it!" (*Guitar World* – June 7, 2024), Snider: "I am a…it? *It's Queen'.*" (*Long Live Queen: Rock Royalty Discuss Freddie, Brian, John & Roger* book – 2018), Ian: "You go back…a sick song.", Bouchard: "If it did…of their career." (*BONZO: 30 Rock Drummers Remember the Legendary John Bonham* book – 2020), Bouchard: "I'd love to…good. Don't worry." (*BONZO: 30 Rock Drummers Remember the Legendary John Bonham* book – 2020), Whitford: "I don't remember…quite a production." (*Aerosmith: Pandora's Box* booklet, 1991), Johnson: "I loved his…by the producer." (*Touched by Magic: The Tommy Bolin Story* book – 2008), Johnson: "It actually made…I'm a Star'." (*Touched by Magic: The Tommy Bolin Story* book – 2008), Bolin: "He did that…the other guy." (*Touched by Magic: The Tommy Bolin Story* book – 2008), Emmett: "I can remember…a professional career." (interview with author – August 7, 2024), Emmett: "If you listen…kind of stuff." (interview with author – August 7, 2024), Emmett: "We bought a…just got rewritten." (interview with author – August 7, 2024), Trunk: "I loved all…the first record." (interview with author – August 12, 2024)

Chapter III: The '80s (Part One)

Van Halen: "I'll never forget…finger I'm using'." (*MusicRadar* – December 26, 2023), Van Halen: "Jimmy Page is…what's the purpose?" (*Guitar World* – January 1981), Savage: "I think it's…by Led Zeppelin." (*Pyromania 40th Anniversary* – 2024), Weiss: "I thought it…of Led Zeppelin." (*MTV Ruled the World: The Early Years of Music Video* book – 2011), Morse: "This album made…as a

SOURCES

teenager." (*Classic Rock* – July 28, 2021), Squier: "I was going...went from there." (*Kerrang!* – July 1-15, 1982), Clarke: "There was so...that whole album." (interview with author – August 5, 2024), Clarke: "Mack was one...very quiet suggestions." (interview with author – August 5, 2024), Clarke: "The night that...never forget that." (interview with author – August 5, 2024), Squier: "I like to...we used it." (*Kerrang!* – December 25-January 7, 1987), Laing: "Bobby was able...that do that." (*BONZO: 30 Rock Drummers Remember the Legendary John Bonham* book – 2020), Clarke – "That was Mack's...was killing it." (interview with author – August 5, 2024), Wall: 'You must have...piss you off?" (*Kerrang!* – November 1-14, 1984), Squier: "Well, I try...Fuck them, man!" (*Kerrang!* – November 1-14, 1984), Clarke: "25 or 30...God bless him." (interview with author – August 5, 2024), Squier: "The whole British...kids like me." (*Circus* – July 31, 1982), Trunk: "Billy Squier is...was so 'Zeppelin-y'." (interview with author – August 12, 2024), Clarke: "I miss him...and on top." (interview with author – August 5, 2024), Benante: "I think Eric...great Kiss record." (*The Eric Carr Story* book – 2011), Jackson: "We ran two...going to sound." (*The Eric Carr Story* book – 2011), Jackson: "And then later...character very clearly." (*The Eric Carr Story* book – 2011), Trunk: "I think Bobby...that Bonham had." (interview with author – August 12, 2024), Jackson: "Now, a debut...almost 100,000 records." (*The Metal Voice* – April 11, 2023), Jackson: "If you look...than anybody else." (WUSB/Stony Brook – December 5, 2023), Jackson: "A lot of...people I knew. (*EveryoneLovesGuitar* – September 14, 2018), Emmett: "A song like...that, for us." (interview with author – August 13, 2024), Plant: "I think it's...17 are OK." (*Creem* – October 1983), Plant: "Because they all...the blues voice." (*Creem* – October 1983), Plant: "If I'm responsible...never saying that." (*Q Magazine* –

165 LED CLONES

March 1988), Gillan: "We had been…to the phrase." (*Songfacts* – August 3, 2020), Plant: "desert island albums selections" (*Globe and Mail* – June 8, 1985), Plant: "I love the…songs without Zeppelin." (*Kerrang!* – June 17-30, 1982), Elliott: "People don't ever…all this bullshit." (*MTV Ruled the World: The Early Years of Music Video* book – 2011), Snider: "I remember being…to *my* music'?" (*Rock Science* – November 22, 2012), Trunk: "I didn't think…fill that sound." (interview with author – August 12, 2024), Plant: "We rehearsed with…Led Zeppelin gigs." (*Q Magazine* – March 1988), Plant: "Live Aid was… this 'My Way'?" (*Rolling Stone* – February 23, 1995), Emmett: "I didn't think…taking a chance." (interview with author – August 7, 2024), Elliott: "It's not really…was technical problems." (*MTV Ruled the World: The Early Years of Music Video* book – 2011), Emmett: "The general public…disappointing. That's heartbreaking." (interview with author – August 7, 2024), Plant: "Jimmy had to… money. I'm off'." (*Rolling Stone* – March 24, 1988), Plant: "Like David Byrne meets Hüsker Dü" (*Rolling Stone* – March 24, 1988), Oliver: "They looked the…turn to dust." (*Kerrang!* – June 4, 1988), Oliver: "If the Live…warm summer evening." (*Kerrang!* – June 4, 1988), Oliver: "Fuck Kingdom Come…I've ever heard." (*Kerrang!* – June 4, 1988), Oliver: "They were in…believe their ears." (*Kerrang!* – June 4, 1988), Trunk: "The common thought…all of that." (interview with author – August 12, 2024), Trunk: "It's funny too…we're seeing now." (interview with author – August 12, 2024)

Chapter IV: The '80s (Part Two)

Russell: "To be honest…all that mattered." (*Kerrang!* – January 16, 1988), Dome: "Jack's voice is…A true star."

SOURCES 166

(*Kerrang!* – October 31, 1987), Dome: "So, what of…the infectious chorus." (*Kerrang!* – October 31, 1987), Niven: "In the early…Willie Dixon was." (interview with author – August 9, 2024), Niven: "'Rock Me' had…still sounds fresh." (interview with author – August 9, 2024), Russell: "I think it's…Aerosmith and Zeppelin." (*Kerrang!* – November 7, 1987), Russell: "It all comes…the fucking blues." (*Kerrang!* – November 7, 1987), Niven: "Jack loved singing…validity to me." (interview with author – August 9, 2024), Niven: "That's a difficult…brick upon brick." (interview with author – August 9, 2024), Niven: "There was a…*than I do*." (interview with author – August 9, 2024), Keifer: "I grew up…and make records." (*Sleaze Roxx* – July 15, 2013), Keifer: "I remember getting…Very inventive record." (*Classic Rock* – December 26, 2020), Sykes: "You see, I…album and ran." (*Earofnewt*, 1989), Coverdale: "As you know…over very well." (*Metal Edge* – no date given), Coverdale: "We were jamming…rest is history." (*Whitesnake Greatest Hits 2022* interview – 2022), Bonutto: "But, but, baby…still be Whitesnake?" (*Kerrang!* – April 2-15, 1987), Coverdale: "The thing is…in and stuff." (*Kerrang!* – April 2-15, 1987), Coverdale: "Yes, but then…of stuff now?" (*Kerrang!* – April 2-15, 1987), Coverdale: "The thing is…in and stuff." (*Kerrang!* – April 2-15, 1987), Coverdale: "Actually, I guess…in the world." (*Hit Parader* – October 1987), Coverdale: "Adrian brought the…to regret later." (*Kerrang!* – March 13, 1993), Benante: "I used to…'Whole Lotta Love'!" (*BONZO: 30 Rock Drummers Remember the Legendary John Bonham* book – 2020), Plant: "I spent so…be Paul Rodgers." (*Kerrang!* – January 23, 1988), Page: "To tell you…a bit cheap." (*Kerrang!* – June 25, 1988), Plant: "I know the…do the talking." (*Chicago Tribune* – March 6, 1988), Coverdale: "There's certainly no…he was starving." (*Far Out* –

167 LED CLONES

December 3, 2021), Coverdale: "There's certainly no…were mostly defensive." (*TeamRock Radio's Classic Rock Magazine Show* – June 19, 2013), Trunk: "I think also…in the blues." (interview with author – August 12, 2024), Chaisson: "Ray [Gillen] was…guy, Michael White!" (interview with author – August 6, 2024)

Chapter V: The '80s (Part Three)

Wolf: "I immediately went…so to write." (*Kerrang!* – March 19, 1988), Kottak: "Funny enough, I…was really magic." (*BraveWords* – October 16, 2018), Kottak: "We went to…a banner day." (*BraveWords* – October 16, 2018), Wall: "What we've got…THE DODDMAN SAME!!" (*Kerrang!* – March 5, 1988), Wall: "As for me…would have puked." (*Kerrang!* – March 5, 1988), Christgau: "I'm not curious…as musical form." (robertchristgau.com – date unknown), Wall: "I wanted to…Kingdom Come yet?" (*Kerrang!* – June 25, 1988), Page: "Kingdom Clone?" (*Kerrang!* – June 25, 1988), Page: "Um, I've heard…back, you know?" (*Kerrang!* – June 25, 1988), Jones: "Ian [Anderson] is…my pet hates." (*Ultimate Guitar* – 2007), Wolf: "This isn't some…sounding like us." (*Kerrang!* – March 19, 1988), Wolf: "Led Zeppelin copied…don't steal parts." (*Kerrang!* – March 19, 1988), Stag: "Every rock drummer…of my influences." (*Kerrang!* – March 19, 1988), Wolf: "You start writing…my own stuff." (*Kerrang!* – March 19, 1988), Kottak: "The first album…odd band out." (*BraveWords* – October 16, 2018), Niven: "I feel a…really rich dessert." (interview with author – August 9, 2024), Niven: "Izzy [Stradlin] was…were more repelled'." (interview with author – August 9, 2024), Trunk: "I worked in…pretty darn cool'." (interview with author – August 12, 2024)

SOURCES 168

Chapter VI: The '80s (Part Four)

Astbury: "We'd already been…and Blue Cheer." (*Rolling Stone* – September 19, 2013), Astbury: "The Cult had…find this guy!" (*Rolling Stone* – September 19, 2013), Astbury: "When we first…want to rock?" (*Rolling Stone* – September 19, 2013), "There was an…t-shirts made up." (*Rolling Stone* – September 19, 2013), Rubin: "We did! We'd…first Zeppelin album." (*Rolling Stone* – September 19, 2013), Rubin: "In the case…rock band recording." (*Conversations with Tyler* – January 18, 2023), Astbury: "I don't think…off with us." (*Kerrang!* – December 5, 1987), Niven: "I really liked…was *the Cult'*." (interview with author – August 9, 2024), Lydon: "I was supposed…beautiful landscaping." (*Classic Rock* – September 4, 2015), Diamond: "Rick definitely came…about that shit'." (*Ultimate Classic Rock* – November 15, 2016), Rubin: "That one was…in that record." (*XXL* – July 2, 2013), Bonham: "I went very…new band, Bonham. (*MTV Rockumentary: Bonham* – 1990), Bonham: "I grew up…we'll disregard it!" (*Kerrang* – October 14, 1989), Bonham: "Something I came…You' really works." (*Kerrang* – October 14, 1989), Bonham: "That track has…Zeppelin influenced me!" (*Kerrang* – October 14, 1989), Plant: "How do I…remove a testicle." (*MTV Rockumentary: Bonham* – 1990), Plant: "When you asked…it home now." (*MTV Rockumentary: Bonham* – 1990), Bonham: "It's pretty tough…kingdom is mine." (*MTV Rockumentary: Bonham* – 1990), Trunk: "The song 'Wait…similar to Zeppelin." (interview with author – August 12, 2024), Sykes: "I never realized…funk really well." (*Kerrang!* – April 29, 1989), Sykes: "When I was…list is endless." (*Kerrang!* – April 29, 1989), Sykes: "I drew from…around these days." (*Kerrang!* – April 29, 1989), Johnson: "A man who…and the Cult." (*Kerrang!* –

169 LED CLONES

April 29, 1989), Johnson: "superb *Led Zep II* sound" (*Kerrang!* – April 29, 1989), Sykes: "It might have…at that time." (*Melodic Rock* – July 1999), Trunk: "Gosh, I love…Jones did not." (interview with author – August 12, 2024), Plant: "I can't blame…um…so pompous." (*Q Magazine* – March 1988)

Chapter VII: The '80s (Part Five)

Chaisson: "I think the…a little bit." (interview with author – August 6, 2024), Chaisson: "Tommy Bolin, Frank…feel' to it." (interview with author – August 6, 2024), Chaisson: "'Winter's Call' I…was in Ozzy." (interview with author – August 6, 2024), Chaisson: "Ray unfortunately gets…would sound good." (interview author – August 6, 2024), Chaisson: "Ray had clearly…stage. His vibrato." (interview with author – August 6, 2024), Gillen: "Humble Pie, Free…from those guys?" (*Kerrang!* – May 27, 1989), Gillen: "While we were…six years ago!" (*Kerrang!* – May 27, 1989), Chaisson: "He's the best…professional that way." (interview with author – August 6, 2024), Gillen: "It took a…bass, and drums." (*Kerrang!* – May 27, 1989), Chaisson: "The triggered part…it less annoying." (interview with author – August 6, 2024), Chaisson: "Yes and no…number of reasons." (interview with author – August 6, 2024), Moore: "'Led Clones' was…the fade out." (*Rockbox* – February 1989), Moore: "It was quite…Real 'Spinal Tap'." (*Kerrang!* – February 11, 1989), Chaisson: "I'm just finishing…'Led Clones' diatribe. (interview with author – August 6, 2024), Emmett: "I think that's…I don't know." (interview with author – August 7, 2024), Trunk: "I was a…go-to for me." (interview with author – August 12, 2024), Trunk: "As time goes…it their own." (interview with author – August 12, 2024), Chaisson: "When you listen…sounding more real."

SOURCES 170

(interview with author – August 6, 2024), Chaisson: "Eric's approach from…it very well." (interview with author – August 6, 2024), Jones: "Bonzo's favorite music…stuff in it." (*MTV Rockumentary: Led Zeppelin* – 1990), Niven: "What Zeppelin had…it was unstoppable." (interview with author – August 9, 2024), Benante: "I think it…top of that." (*BONZO: 30 Rock Drummers Remember the Legendary John Bonham* book – 2020), Benante: "I heard two…green sparkle kit." (*BONZO: 30 Rock Drummers Remember the Legendary John Bonham* book – 2020), Ocheltree: "He listened to…jazz-fusion, Latin music." (*BONZO: 30 Rock Drummers Remember the Legendary John Bonham* book – 2020), Ocheltree: "Expression – I think…had a lesson." (*BONZO: 30 Rock Drummers Remember the Legendary John Bonham* book – 2020), Rarebell: "I think that…two bass drums." (*BONZO: 30 Rock Drummers Remember the Legendary John Bonham* book – 2020), Rarebell: "But nobody has…so to speak." (*BONZO: 30 Rock Drummers Remember the Legendary John Bonham* book – 2020), Benante: "Tried to do…vocally and musically." (*BONZO: 30 Rock Drummers Remember the Legendary John Bonham* book – 2020), Emmett: "The things about… *it was genius*." (interview with author – August 7, 2024), Aronoff: "Cozy Powell was…it real good." (*BONZO: 30 Rock Drummers Remember the Legendary John Bonham* book – 2020), Benante: "I think Cozy…arms stand up" (*BONZO: 30 Rock Drummers Remember the Legendary John Bonham* book – 2020), Trunk: "You mentioned Bobby…in my opinion." (interview with author – August 12, 2024)

Chapter VIII: The '90s

Plant: "It's lack of…most obvious thing." (*Kerrang!* – June 9, 1990), Plant: "People like Faith…of so many..."

171 LED CLONES

(*Kerrang!* – June 9, 1990), Plant: "I think their…heard in years." (*Kerrang!* – June 9, 1990), Beezer: "They came out…they're really good'!" (*Grunge Is Dead: The Oral History of Seattle Rock Music* book – 2009), Moody: "I saw one…back to back." *Grunge Is Dead: The Oral History of Seattle Rock Music* book – 2009), Hallerman: "Kim [Thayil] did…influence for them." (*Grunge Is Dead: The Oral History of Seattle Rock Music* book – 2009), Thayil: "We did the…won them over." (*The Faith No More & Mr. Bungle Companion* book – 2013), Cornell: "It was kind…pass over it." (*The Howard Stern Show* – 2011), Chaisson: "Chris Cornell obviously…Chris Cornell fan." (interview with author – August 6, 2024), Channing: "It was Dale…together, I supposed." (*BONZO: 30 Rock Drummers Remember the Legendary John Bonham* book – 2020), Channing: "We were always…for the drums." (*BONZO: 30 Rock Drummers Remember the Legendary John Bonham* book – 2020), Plant: "I've never seen…catch them again." (*Raw* – July 6, 1994), Stevens: "We had always…never seen before." (*A Devil on One Shoulder and an Angel on the Other: The Story of Shannon Hoon and Blind Melon* book – 2008), Page: "In the Zeppelin…orchestrated-guitar element." (*Rolling Stone* – December 6, 2012), Kretz: "Definitely. Because Brendan…were putting together." (*BONZO: 30 Rock Drummers Remember the Legendary John Bonham* book – 2020), Kretz: "Whenever you try…just for fun?" (*BONZO: 30 Rock Drummers Remember the Legendary John Bonham* book – 2020), Kravitz: "I went to…on the run'." (*Rolling Stone* – October 9, 2018), Kravitz: "That song was…what I had." (*Rolling Stone* – October 9, 2018), Strauss: "So you don't…'Living Loving Maid'?" (*Rolling Stone* – November 30, 1995), Kravitz: "No, I mean…talk about it." (*Rolling Stone* – November 30, 1995), Kravitz: "I was doing…friends ever since." (*Classic Rock* – May 31, 2024), Claypool: "The

SOURCES 172

Brown Album...with the percussion." (*Primus, Over the Electric Grapevine: Insight into Primus and the World of Les Claypool* book – 2014), Mantia: "Les's whole concept...muffled, compressed sound." (*Primus, Over the Electric Grapevine: Insight into Primus and the World of Les Claypool* book – 2014), Coverdale: "In essence, Jimmy...with personal circumstances." (*Kerrang!* – March 13, 1993), Page: "After the *Outrider*...working with David?'." (*Kerrang!* – March 13, 1993), Page: "We just went...going to be..." ." (*Kerrang!* – March 13, 1993), Coverdale: "Led Snake." (*Kerrang!* – March 13, 1993), Endino: "They were playing...pretty good record." (*Survival of the Fittest: Heavy Metal in the 1990's* book – 2015), Endino: "Wow! That was...an interesting experience." (*Survival of the Fittest: Heavy Metal in the 1990's* book – 2015), Emmett: "That to me...it a run'." (interview with author – August 7, 2024), Trunk: "I liked it...to be that." (interview with author – August 12, 2024), Chaisson: "I actually liked...work – go figure." (interview with author – August 6, 2024), Hotten: "*Coverdale Page* is...most often majestic." (*Kerrang!* – March 13, 1993), Coverdale: "I was very...lot of fun." (*107.7 The Bone's Lamont & Tonelli* – 2021), Plant: "I would have...couldn't go ahead." (*Rolling Stone* – February 23, 1995), Plant: "My only problem...know each other." (*Rolling Stone* – February 23, 1995), Page: "The MTV thing...from Day One." (*Rolling Stone* – February 23, 1995), Jones: "I've read what...a bit odd." (*Rolling Stone* – February 23, 1995)

Chapter IX: The 21st Century

White: "That's the main...Willie Johnson recording." (*Light and Shade: Conversations with Jimmy Page* book – 2012), Stockdale: "I lived in...in the harbor." (*Songfacts* – October

173 LED CLONES

5, 2015), Stockdale: "What I am...man! That sticks!" (*Songfacts* – October 5, 2015), Stockdale: "And there's a...as you can." (*Songfacts* – October 5, 2015), Stockdale: "Every has to...all to happen." (*Songfacts* – October 5, 2015), Stockdale: "I think I'd...in small doses." (*Entertainment Weekly* – May 31, 2006), Holiday: "Growing up in...into my 20's." (*Tidal* – February 25, 2015), Monahan: "I was in...shown up earlier." (*Ultimate Classic Rock* – May 24, 2016), Monahan: "When we learned...learn the rest." (*Ultimate Classic Rock* – May 24, 2016), Monahan: "We went in...was pretty interesting." (*Ultimate Classic Rock* – May 24, 2016), Monahan: "Every part of...he's so great." (*Ultimate Classic Rock* – May 24, 2016), Jake Kiszka: "We all share...and Robby Krieger." (*BraveWords* – September 6, 2017), Jake Kiszka: "As for Led...and banjo playing." (*Guitar Player* – August 22, 2023), Lawson: "The debut album...previous retro-fetishism." (*Pitchfork* – October 23, 2018), Lawson: "Greta Van Fleet...they arrested themselves." (*Pitchfork* – October 23, 2018), Lawson: "They make music...Zeppelin often were." (*Pitchfork* – October 23, 2018), Lawson: "And at least...literary-fantasy songs." (*Pitchfork* – October 23, 2018), Josh Kiszka: "Obviously we hear...Let's move on." (*Rolling Stone* – January 19, 2019), Plant: "There is a...going to do?" (*The Project* – March 28, 2018), White: "They're three Polish...shit goes away." (*Rolling Stone* – July 15, 2019), Benante: "They're young kids...on guys...*stop*'." (*BONZO: 30 Rock Drummers Remember the Legendary John Bonham* book – 2020), Trunk: "Zeppelin to this...one immensely interesting." (interview with author – August 12, 2024), Notto: "'Stairway to Heaven'...to that stuff." (*100 Percent Rock* – February 2020), Chaisson: "The Atomic Kings...a 'Kashmir' feel!" (interview with author – August 6, 2024), Clarke: "I love Greta...years now, actually." (interview with author –

SOURCES 174

August 5, 2024), Emmett: "Greta Van Fleet…down the line." (interview with author – August 7, 2024), Niven: "Oh God…*stop*…studio sound.' *Boring*." (interview with author – August 9, 2024), Chaisson: "Greta Van Fleet…up to it." (interview with author – August 6, 2024), Trunk: "To me, Greta…world, for sure." (interview with author – August 12, 2024), Trunk: "I think the…that autonomy today." (interview with author – August 13, 2024)

Chapter X: Zeppelin Cloned Others?

Ocheltree: "I've got a…that Max wrote." (*BONZO: 30 Rock Drummers Remember the Legendary John Bonham* book – 2020), Plant: "There are zillions…unpleasant for everybody." (*Loose Ends* – November 20, 2021), Niven: "People like Page…on *Zeppelin I*." (interview with author – August 9, 2024), Trunk: "Most people know…a little bit." (interview with author – August 12, 2024), Emmett: "Zeppelin themselves got…*do it too'.*" (interview with author – August 7, 2024), Fricke: "What's your opinion…a different tangent." (*Rolling Stone* – March 24, 1988), Plant: "Maybe he ought…own riffs then." *Rolling Stone* – March 24, 1988)

Chapter XI: Why So Many in the '80s?

Emmett: "No, I don't…in the guts'?" (interview with author – August 7, 2024), Niven: "Timing. I think…a similar sound." (interview with author – August 9, 2024), Trunk: "Well, I think…a similar sound." (interview with author – August 13, 2024), Emmett: "I liked them…grow from there." (interview with author – August 7, 2024), Bonham: "As I've gotten…you, to everybody." (*Long Island Pulse* –

175 LED CLONES

May 25, 2016), Trunk: "You can go…blatant is it'?" (interview with author – August 12, 2024)

Other Books by Greg Prato

Music

A Devil on One Shoulder and an Angel on the Other: The Story of Shannon Hoon and Blind Melon

Touched by Magic: The Tommy Bolin Story

Grunge Is Dead: The Oral History of Seattle Rock Music

No Schlock...Just Rock! (A Journalistic Journey: 2003-2008)

MTV Ruled the World: The Early Years of Music Video

The Eric Carr Story

Too High to Die: Meet the Meat Puppets

The Faith No More & Mr. Bungle Companion

Overlooked/Underappreciated: 354 Recordings That Demand Your Attention

Over the Electric Grapevine: Insight into Primus and the World of Les Claypool

Punk! Hardcore! Reggae! PMA! Bad Brains!

Iron Maiden: '80 '81

Survival of the Fittest: Heavy Metal in the 1990s

Scott Weiland: Memories of a Rock Star

German Metal Machine: Scorpions in the '70s

The Other Side of Rainbow

Shredders!: The Oral History of Speed Guitar (And More)

The Yacht Rock Book: The Oral History of the Soft, Smooth Sounds of the 60s, 70s, and 80s

100 Things Pearl Jam Fans Should Know & Do Before They Die

The 100 Greatest Rock Bassists

Long Live Queen: Rock Royalty Discuss Freddie, Brian, John & Roger

King's X: The Oral History

Facts on Tracks: Stories Behind 100 Rock Classics

Dark Black and Blue: The Soundgarden Story

Take It Off: Kiss Truly Unmasked

A Rockin' Rollin' Man: Bon Scott Remembered

Avatar of the Electric Guitar: The Genius of Jimi Hendrix

BONZO: 30 Rock Drummers Remember the Legendary John Bonham

John Winston Ono Lennon

Shannon

Iconic Guitar Gear

A+ Albums: The Stories Behind 50 Rock Classics (Vol. I), 1970-1982

A+ Albums: The Stories Behind 50 Rock Classics (Vol. II), 1982-2000

Lanegan

The 100 Greatest Songs of Heavy Metal (eBook)

The 100 Greatest Songs of Punk Rock (eBook)

I ♡ GRUNGE: 'GRUNGE IS DEAD' OUTTAKES

50 Rock Lists + surprise twists

World Infestation: The Ratt Story

Sports

Sack Exchange: The Definitive Oral History of the 1980s New York Jets

Dynasty: The Oral History of the New York Islanders, 1972-1984

Just Out of Reach: The 1980s New York Yankees

The Seventh Year Stretch: New York Mets, 1977-1983

Butt Fumbles, Fake Spikes, Mud Bowls & Heidi Games: The Top 100 Debacles of the New York Jets

Hapless Islanders: The Story Behind the New York Islanders' Infamous 1972-73 Season

Made in the USA
Middletown, DE
23 October 2024